ABU TO UDAIPUR

Celestial Simla

TO

City of Sunrise

By

Jodh Singh Mehta

B.A., LL.B., R.A.S. (Retd.)

Author of 'Rover Scouting', (Hindi), 'The Fort of Chittor' (English), 'Chittorgarh' (Hindi), 'A Brief History and Administration of the Mewar' (English), 'Adinivasi Bhil' (Hindi) and 'Chittorgarh' (English)

With a Foreword By

Dr. Daulat Singh Kothari

Chairman, University Grants Commission

MOTILAL BANARSIDASS

DELHI :: VARANASI :: PATNA

©MOTILAL BANARSIDASS
Bungalow Road, Jawaharnagar, Delhi-7
Chowk, Varanasi (U. P.)
Ashok Raj Path, Bankipur, Patna (Bihar)

First Edition
1970

Printed in India by Shantilal Jain, at Shri Jainendra Press, Bungalow Road, Jawaharngar, Delhi-7, and published by Sundarlal Jain, Motilal Banarsidass, Bungalow Bungalow Road, Jawahar Nagar, Delhi-7

FOREWORD

Shri Jodh Singh Mehta, the unassuming, careful and scholarly author of this publication has placed us under his debt by providing a splendid account of the famous and hallowed temples in the Udaipur—Mt. Abu area, and also of other monuments of outstanding art and technical excellence and places of scenic beauty unsurpassed anywhere. The book is fascinating and eminently readable. It would be of value to those interested in places of worship and historic monuments and would add very much to the enjoyment, appreciation and understanding of visitors and tourists going to Rajasthan.

New Delhi
March 19, 1969

D. S. Kothari
Chairman
University grants Commission

PREFACE

Mount Abu is known as 'The Olympus of India'. Between the Himalayas on the north and the Nilgiris on the South, this is the only high mountain which abounds in green shrubberies, tall trees and celestial shrines. Its natural environment attracts the visitors from far and near; its rich products and variegated medicinal plants are both famous and important. Above all, the antiquity and architectural beauty of its Delwada Jain temples, afford a big source of our country's high culture and craftsmanship.

In the vicinity of Abu and further beyond it, we come across many places of profound peace, pleasure and pilgrimage of all the important sects of India. About 200 miles east of Abu, lies Udaipur, 'The Venice of India'—a gem of Rajasthan encircled by lofty Aravalli hills and beset with enchanting lovely lakes. Near about this 'City of Sunrise' is situated Jaisamand, one of the biggest artificial lakes of the World and further to the north-east is Chittorgarh—"The cradle of chivalry and culture", telling the stories of heroic deeds, performed on its sacred soil, to preserve and protect the independence of the country against the foreign invasions. Who does not know Kumbha and Pratap, Karmashah and Bhamashah, Padmini and Meera who along with a galaxy of its brave and meritorious sons and daughters, sacrifiiced every thing for the maintenance of faith and fidelity. In front of it, flows the river Gambhiri which has the civilisation of one lakh years, on its banks. Seven miles from it, are seen the ruins of ancient Nagari—the old republic of India, presenting the relics of the earliest age.

The notable places described in this book are rich in antiquity, art and culture. Besides this, they are of great interest to the students of History, Archaeology and Indology. Moreover, many of the places bear religious significance which lend spiritual background amongst the natural surroundings. Inspired by natural and super-natural, historical and pre-historical association of this part of our country, I have attempted to write this book and named it as Abu to Udaipur—'Celestial Simla' to 'City of Sunrise'.

Abu, Ambaji, Ranakpur, Charbhuja, Nathdwara and Rikhabdev (Kesariyaji), are important holy places which attract a large number of persons, every year, from the different parts of our country. There are others like Chandrāvati, Munghthala (near Abu Road), Ahad (Udaipur). Nagda, Nagri, Chittorgarh, and even Abu which trace their origin from very old times and they are famous historically as well as for their antiquity. Abu, Udaipur and Chittorgarh, are well-renowned places for the tourists also. While visiting the celestial shrines, with their ornamental carvings, we come across so many idols of different kinds of faith, Jain, Vaishnava, Shaiva, and Shākta and also some portrait sculptures as well as bronze images which afford ample opportunity to the students of Iconography, Archaeology, Architecture and Sculpture, for further research and exploration. In the natural environment and spiritual atmosphere, stand these man-made creations which provide peace and pleasure to the tourists and travellers coming from hurly-burly life of the modern cities and towns. I have appended also the life-sketches of eminent persons, Vimal Shah and Vastupal Tejpal who had created heaven upon earth, at holy Abu, about whom many persons are ignorant. They are the historical figures who had played conspicuous part both in war and peace but they have not come into lime-light. To illuminate their lives, is to disclose the inner feelings of their hearts which invoked them to create marvellous monuments of beauty and bounty, unsurpassed by any other works of this kind.

While eulogizing the lives of these great men, we should not forget about the architects and artists who culled out such heavenly abodes, upon the earth with the aid of their chisel from marble and stone. The lives of Sutradhar Kirtidhar of a village near Badnagar (Gujarat), Shabhan Dev of Sompura, and Deepa Shilpi of Nath School of Sculpture, Chittorgarh who constructed Vimal Vasahi, Luna Vasahi and Ranakpur temples, are in dark. At present time also, there are a few Sompura Shilpis, the chief among them being Shri Amritlal Moolchand Trivedi, who have renovated and repaired some parts of Delwada Jain temples who have exhibited skilful craftsmanship. The art of metal-casting, was prevalent, in Rajasthan and Gujarat, during the mediaeval period and we find the names of Sutradhar Lumbu, Lampu of Dungerpur (V.S.1518), Sutradhar Deva (Sutār of Mehsana North—Gujarat V.S.1525) and Sutradhar Haridas who had casted beautiful bronze images of Chaumuk temple Achalgarh and Pittalhar temple, Delwala. It becomes, therefore, imperative upon us, to find out the material for drawing out the pen-pictures of these artists and skilmen who have created such lovely and magnificent masterpieces of art and crafts, out of marble and metal.

In writing the chapters on Abu, I was mostly guided by the works Abu Part I, II and III, written by late Muni Jayant Vijayaji and the English translation of Abu Part I, namely Holy Abu, by Dr. Umakant Premanand Shah. Annals and Antiquities of Rajasthan by Col. Tod and Rajputana Ka Itihasa and Sirohi Rajya ka Itihasa, by Gauri Shanker Heera Chand Ojha, were helpful for giving some references in the book. Bibliography of the other books consulted has been given along with the names of the authors. I am greatly indebted to the authors of all the books which I have consulted. At the same time, I cannot forget, to thank Shri T.C. Aneja M.A. (English), the former teacher of Tibetan School, Delwada, Abu, who took pains to go through the manuscript of this book and gave some useful suggestions.

In rendering this book illustrative, for proper appreciation of the important pieces of art and architecture, I have received great help from sundry sources. First of all, I am much grateful to Sheth Kasturbhai Lalbhai, Ahmedabad who has very readily put at my disposal, the photo-set of Ranakpur Temples and permitted me to reproduce the post-card size printed photos of Mount Abu and Ranakpur Temples which are a gift to him from Dr. Robert Kappeli Bale of Ciba Company, Switzerland who holds copyright. The Archaeological Survey of India, has copyright over the printed postcard size photo-set of Chittorgarh and the Director General, Archaeological Survey of India, has very kindly allowed me to reproduce this photoset, for which I am indebted to him. In this connection, I am much obliged to Shah Fakir Bhai of Ahmedabad who has offered me the photo-set of Chittorgarh. I express my indebtedness both to the Director and the Deputy Director, Public Relations Department, Rajasthan, Jaipur who supplied me with some fine photo copies of Abu, for use in this book. I would like to thank some other persons also, who helped me in procurement of some nice photos with them. Shri Balwant Sinha Mehta, Ex-M.P. gave me, the photo picture of Rana Pratap, riding on his charger Chetak, the life-size statue at Pratap Smarak, Udaipur. Similarly Shri Surajmal K. Shah, Chairman, Swetamber Nakoda Parshvanath temples, Shri Veer Chand Siraya, Secretary Shri Jain Swetamber Tirth Shri Kareda Parshvanath. Trust Udaipur, and Shri Fateh Lal Manawat of Shri

Padmanath Swamiji Tirth, Udaipur offered me the photographs of the temples under their charge.

I am highly indebted to Shri Sunder Lal Jain, of the famous firm Motilal Banarsidass Indological Publishers and Booksellers of India, Delhi, for readily agreeing to publish this book, at my request.

Lastly, I am very deeply indebted to Dr. D. S. Kothari, Chairman, University Grants Commission, India, Delhi, a well known scientist and educationist to find time from his busy hours to write a foreword to this work at my personal request.

Delwada S. Jain
Temples, Mount Abu
Dated 10-2-1969

Jodh Singh Mehta

BIBLIOGRAPHY

(*Gujarati books*)

1. Tirth-Raj Abu, Abu Bhag Pahelo —*Late Muni Jayant Vijayji.*
2. Shri—Arbuda—Prachina—Jain—Lekh—Samdoh—Abu Bhag Bijo —*do*—
3. Achalgadh—Abu, Bhag Trijo —*do*—
4. Vimal Shah —*Dhirajlal Tokursi, Ahmedabad.*
5. Gujarat no Veer Mantri Tejpal —*Pt. Lalchandra B. Gandhi*
6. Prachina Jain Tirth Kumbhariya (unpublished) —*Chandulal Lallubhai Shah, Ahmedabad*
7. Shri Vastupal Charitra —*Shri Jina Harsha Gani*

(*Hindi books*)

8. Bhagwan Parasnath ki Parampara Ka Itihasa Vol I —*Late Muni Gyan Sunderji*
9. Shri Merutungacharya Prabandh chintamani, Sanskrit Granth, Compiled by Muni Jinavijayaji, Hindi Bhashantar —*Pt. Hazari Prasadji Dwivedi*
10. Rajputana Ka Itihasa —*Late Pt. Gauri Shankar Heerachand Ojha*
11. Sirohi Rajya Ka Itihasa

12. Punya Bhoomi Ka Punya Smarana —*Shri Rajendra Shankar Bhatt*
13. Jheelon Ki Nagari —*Goyal Brothers*
14. Abu (Hindi) Prathama Bhaga —*Late Muni Shri Jayant Vijayaji*
15. Shodha Patrika, September, 1960. —*Sahitya Sansthan Udaipur Rajasthan Vidhya Peeth*

(*English books*)

16. Holy Abu—Muni Jayant Vijayaji —*Translated by Dr. Umakant Premanand Shah.*
17. Annals and Antiquities of Rajasthan; 1957 edition --*Cal. Tod.*
18. Mount Abu —*Late S. B. Singh,*
19. Mount Abu—The Olympus of Rajasthan —*Om Prakash Gupta.*
20. Udaipur Invites —*President, City Corporation, Udaipur.*
21. Glimpses of Mewar —*Dr. Motilal Menaria, Udaipur.*
22. A Pocket Guide to the Natural Sceneries of Mewar —*Sarup Lall Sanādhya, Udaipur.*
23. The Temples at Ranakpur —*Sheth Anandji Kalyanji,*
24. A Glimpse of World Famous Delwara Temples —*Compiled by B. L. Sureemal*
25. Chittorgarh—Cradle of Chivalry and Culture —*Balwant Sinha Mehta and Jodh Singh Mehta,*
26. A Brief History and Administration of Mewar. —*Jodh Singh Mehta, Udaipur.*

CONTENTS

'Celestial Simla' to 'The City of Sunrise'

Abu to Udaipur

The City of Sunrise—Udaipur

The excursions from Udaipur

CELESTIAL SIMLA

ABU

The ancient name—Arbudgiri or Arbudachal

Abu is famous as 'Arbudgiri' or Arbudachal in the ancient Hindu and Jain Scriptures. On this mount, a Kamadhenu or a heavenly cow of Vasishta Rishi, fell into a deep pit which was said to have been filled up, by placing a serpent named Arbuda, on the back of which, came Nandivardhan, the son of the Himalayas. Thus, it came to be known as Arbudgiri, after the name of the serpent Arbuda. The Jains interpret that Arbuda or one hundred crores of Munis, came over to this hill for practising penance as well as for having Darshana (look) of the Jain Gods—Rishabhdeva and Neminath. There is also another Jain belief that whosoever makes offering of any article, to the temple of Lord Rishabhdeva, it transforms Arbuda-guna or a hundred crores times, for him, in the next birth.

Pre-historic references

Whatever may be the origin of the name of this hill, it is an undoubted fact that Abu is considered as a sacred place by Hindus, Jains, Shāktas and Shaivas—the followers of the principal religions of India. There are many important places on the mount, associated with the names of Gods, Goddesses, Rishis and Munis, Vishnu and Raghunath, Rishabhdev and Neminath, Achleshvar and Neelakanth, Kanyakumari and Adhardevi. On the hill itself, there is an old place called 'Devāngan' or 'the courtyard of the gods'. It is held by the Jains that Bharat Chakravarti, erected here, in the very ancient past, a big temple, installing the idol of Lord Rikhabdev, his father and first Tirthankar. It is also said that Lord Mahavir, the last Tirthankar, paid visit to this hill as a Jain saint, before attainment of his salvation.

The mention of 'Arbuda' is found in some of the oldest hymns of the Rigveda (X. 68.12 and I 51.61). The place was inhabited by the Bhillalas—the aboriginal tribes. The Nagas, too, migrated to this mountain, at the time of Snake-sacrifice by the king Janmejaya and lived in the caves of this mountain, worshipping the goddess Durga in 610-800 B.C. In Mahabharat, the reference of Vasishtashram or the hermitage of Rishi Vasishta, at Abu, is found. In the older Puranas, the Abu area is considered as Aparānta or Western circle coast of India. It was later ruled by the Parmar Kings—the Feudatories of the Solanki rulers of ancient Chandravati Nagari (some four miles from Abu Road). Magasthenes, the well-known Greek ambassador, in the court of Chandra-Gupta Maurya, described it as 'Mount Capitalia' with gold silver mines near it.

History

The earliest reference in history, is found in the seventh century when samant Rajjil—the son of Vajrabhat and a feudatory Chief of king Varmlat of Bhillamala (modern Bhinmal) had been ruling over Abu. Then came the Paramars, with Dhumraj as the original person in 961 A.D., Dharnivah, the descendant of Dhumraj, became subservient to Mulraj solanki of Gujarat. Dhundhuk, the grandson of Dharnivah, fled towards Chittor and Malwa and later re-established at Chandravati after accepting the terms of Bhimdeva, the solanki king of Gujarat, on persuasion of VIMAL SHAH, the minister of Bhimdev. In 1031 A.D., Vimal Shah built Vimal Vasahi—one of the most wonderful temples of the world, at Delwara (Abu). In the line of Dhundhuk, Dharavarsh was prominent and powerful whose statue with bow and arrow, is found erected at Achalgarh, on this hill. Dharavarsh, was followed by his son, Som Singh and during his time, Vastupal and Tejpal, both brothers and the ministers of the King Viradhaval of Gujarat, constructed another marvellous shrine, by the name of Luna-Vasahi, in 1231 A.D. at Delwara. The last Parmar ruler of Abu was killed by Deora Chauhan Chief Rao Lumba in 1311 A.D. He established his capital at Chandravati which was later shifted to Sirohi in 1405 A.D., by his descendant Rao Sahasmal. For short duration, Abu was occupied by Rana Kumbha of Mewar who construced the fort 'Achalgarh'. He was repulsed, by Rao Lakha of Sirohi. It was from the hill of Abu that the successors of Lumba, could succeed in withstanding the Muslim and Mughal onslaughts and maintained the independence of Sirohi, a contemporary of Maharana Pratap, in the battle of Dattani in 1583 A.D. "Therefore, we find that Abu, remained a strategic hill—a point of vantage against the foreign invasions on Sirohi.'

With the advent of the Britishers, in India, the Sirohi rulers made treaty with the British Government. In 1822 A.D. Col. Tod came to Abu. As he says 'He discovered Abu.' In 1845 A.D., the headquarters of Political Agent for Rajaputana was established here and a treaty was signed with Rao Shiva-Singh of Sirohi. On the 6th October 1917, a permanent lease was given to the British Government, on payment of subsidy of Rs. 27,000 to the Sirohi Ruler. On the 6th July 1947, the area of Abu was retroceded to the Sirohi Ruler. After the independence of the country, on 15th August 1947, Abu came under the Bombay Govt., on 25th January 1950 and ultimately it was amalgamated into Rajasthan state, on 1st November 1956, at the recommendation of the States' Reorganisation Commission. It is now the Head-Quarters of the Sub-Divisional Officer, within Sirohi District and a summer resort of the Governor of Rajasthan.

Geography

Abu Mount is situated towards south and south-west, of Rajasthan. The hill forms a part of Aravalli range, but is detached from it by a narrow valley of some seven miles across, through which flows the river Bānas. It is composed of the archaean granites, schists and limestones. Fragments of mica and hard crystalline lime-stones are also to be found in different parts of this mountain. It has a long and narrow shape, running from south-east to north-east. Its top is spreading out into a fine plateau, 12 miles in length and 3 miles in breadth and nearly 4,000 ft. above sea-level. The base of the mountain is 20 miles long and 8 miles broad, at its widest part. The highest peak, is Gurshikar which is 5,650 ft, above sea-level. It is the highest point between the Himalayas and the Nilgiris. It is situated in 24°-36′ North longitude and 72°-43′ East latitude. The mean temperature is about 70°F. while the average rainfall is about 68 inches. The plateau is swept by cool and refreshing air which vigorates the health of its inhabitants. The hill-sides of the mountain, are covered with rich foliage of various kinds of trees, chief being mangoes, date-palms and bamboos. There are many kinds of wild shrubs and flower-plants scattered here and there on the slopes of the mountain, the prominent being Karuruda (Carissa caranass), Champa (Michelia Champaca) Jasmine and Kara (Strobilanthus callosus). Mogra and Ketki are abundant near Vasishta-Ashram. Jamun is a common tree, Kachnār, is another handsome tree, here. There are to be found many kinds of herbs which are used in the preparation of Ayurvedic medicines. The tigers and panthers, have been rare, these days. Sloth bears and black-faced monkeys are common. Fish and crabs are plenty in streams and tanks. Cobras, Kraits, Russels and Echis-vipers are four kinds of snakes which are to be seen. It is visited by the song-birds and butterflies which are numerous and varied. There are three kinds of bees and they are easy to be domesticated. There is also a bee-farming centre on the hill, run by Rajasthan Khadi and village Industries Board.

Architecture and Sculpture

The architecture and sculpture of Abu, are well known in the World, as represented in the magnificent marble Jain temples of Delwada, built in the eleventh and thirteenth centuries. This art flourished profusely in the mediaeval period of Indian-History between 1100-1400 A.D. It represents a typical school of art of Gujarat which can be traced to Brahminical temple architecture which laid down that temple architecture should contain sculptures representing Apsaras, Siddhas and various designs. Again the Rangamandaps (Central courtyards), entrance gates, Torans (arches) may belong to different sects like Brahaminical, Jain or Swaminarayan but in all of them, the hand of Sompura sculptures working behind all of them can be discerned. The same style of art and architecture existed in Gujarat, Malwa, Mewar and even upto East Khandesh. It was a rich and well-developed art, not identifying with the political boundary of Gujarat of today. The cultural boundaries of Gujarat extended to Rajasthan also. It is said to have belonged to Rajasthan Mandal. In Rajasthan, there were two different Schools of Sculpture, founded by two famous architects. Madan and Nath both brothers, living at Chittorgarh, during the times of Rana Kumbha who himself was a great author on works of Sculpture. 'The Tower of Victory' at Chittor, built by

Rana Kumbha, is the best living specimen of the former school while the famous Jain Temples of Ranakpur belong to the latter school. Both the brothers, and Govind (the son of Nath) wrote good many books on Sculpture as well as on architecture. The art of Modhera and Chandravati, is inherited from Ranakpur. Thus, the influence of Rajasthan School of atchitecture spread out, in Gujarat also. Independently also, Gujarat had its own class of famous artisans and sculptors who were living near about Badnagar and they constructed huge and massive forts in the Southern India. Among these architects, was Kirtidhar who planned and built, the famous shrine at Delwada namely Vimal Vasahi, in the first half of the eleventh century. "The Delwara temples display a profuse use of marble for architecture. The dancing figures on the ruins of the Rudramahalya at Siddhapur appear again on the pillars at Delwara near Mt. Abu". In the ceilings of the Delwada Jain Temples, are carved out the scenes of Hindu mythology, side by side with the ancient episodes related in the Jain Scriptures. This fact leads us to believe that Jainism made great contribution towards Gujarat architecture in a very unconventional or catholic manner. It represents a typical school or art of Gujarat. Vimal Vasahi, built by Vimal Shah at Delwada, is an indispensable record for student of Jain Iconography and Luna-Vasahi, in an improvement of this art, after a period of two hundred years. Though the latter is smaller in size than the former, yet it presents the detailed and different variety of carvings. The male and female figures, in these two temples, are the best human figures ever depicted, perhaps, in the whole of the World. The dexterious delineation and workmanship that we notice on human figures, animals, flower designs, gods and goddesses as well as on the different types of pillars, Rangamandaps and arches, of these Delwada temples, would not be found anywhere else. The female figures have been chisselled out, according to the ancient texts of Indian dancing. The eight poses and eight kinds of dances, have been shown prominently. On the carvings of the massive pillars adorned with the rich varieties of bands, are to be seen the coquettish looking female figures, in varied actions and poses. Some of them are holding flutes or drums while others are carrying water-jugs in their hands while bend of their waists is abundantly charming to the onlookers. These two temples, are the most wonderful specimen of Indian architecture and sculpture. Col. Tod, the famous historian, says that "This temple is the best throughout India and it cannot be compared except with Taj Mahal." He further remarks that the dome in the centre is the most stirking feature and magnificent piece of work and has a pendant, cylindrical in form and about three feet in length that is a perfect gem and which where it drops from the ceiling appears like a cluster of half-disclosed lotus whose cups are so thin, so transparent and so accurately wrought that it fixes the eyes in admiration."

Col. Eraskin, describes these temples in his own way. He writes 'The amount of ornamental detail spread over these structures in the minutely carved decoration of ceilings, doorways, pillars, panels and niches, is simply marvellous, while the crisp translucent shell-like treatment of the marble surpasses anything seen elsewhere, and some of the designs are just dreams of beauty.' Fergusson, the eminent Archaeologist relates that "It hangs from the centre more like a lustre of crystal drops than a solid mass of marble and is finished with a delicacy of detail and appropriateness of ornament which is probably unsurpassed by any similar example to be found anywhere else". Another famous historian, Gaurishanker Hira Chand Ojha, narrates that there is no temple in India which can be compared with that Temple (Vimal Vasahi) in art and workmanship. The sculpture of these beautiful temples, can only be better appreciated by expert artists but a layman can follow up, the dress, rites and customs, trade and commerce, battle-scenes and royal processions, courts and countries, animals and birds, so nicely depicted inside the temples. In a nutshell, the Delwada Jain Temples are not only the holy places but they are also an open university, perpetuating the study of History, Sociology, Art and Culture of Western India.

Again, near Kanya Kumari, adjacent to these temples, there is a Vishnu Temple. Further, towards the west, there are lying the ruins of older Shaiva temples. The whole area is considered to be once a flourishing Brahminical Shaivite site. In the Vishnu shrine, there are post-Gupta sculptures of three Matrikas and a fourth of Surya (Sun-God). A sculpture of Vishnu, lying on the Sheshnag (serpent) is of earlier age. In Kanya Kumari, there is another matrika of the same age and a figure of standing Parvati, belonging to the 9th or 10th century A.D. This old site Vaishnava and Shaiva shrines, seems to be of the period between the fifth to eleventh centuries A.D. "The discovery of these ancient places throws a new light on the cultural history of Gujrat and reveals for us some of the most important specimens of sculptured art of Gujarat in the Gupta and Post-Gupta age."

In the Mediaeval period down upto the 17th century, we find the art of metal-casting in developed state, in Gujarat and Rajasthan. The rich Parikar of Pittalhar Jain temple of Delwada, the magnitude of the main idols of Shri Adinath in Achalgarh temples and another of the same type in these temples installed in V.S. 1518 and cast at Dungarpur (Rajasthan) are said to be the excellent specimens of brass images of those times in whole of India.

Archaeology

The Jain, Shaiva and Vishu temples of Abu, provide a vast treasure to the students of Archaeology. The human figures of ancient and mediaeval times, carved out on the black and white marble stones, immortalise the history not only of Abu but also of Gujarat and Rajasthan. The inscriptions found here and there, on the mountain and near about it, throw a flood of light, on the family trees of the princes, ministers and prominent persons, their names and surnames, trade and commerce and other social trends of those times. The pioneer work in this direction, was done by the late Jain Muni Shri Jayant Vijayaji who deciphered 664 inscriptions of the Jain temples of Abu, the transcriptions of them being published in the book Shri Arbuda Prāchin Jain Lekh Samdoha." This book reveals that Shravakas or Jain laymen of particular sub-caste, belonged to particular gaccha or the order of monks. The epithets 'Maham' 'Thākur' or 'Thé' and 'Sheśti' or Shri or 'Sā' were prefixed against the names of ministers, Jagirdars and businessmen respectively. The oldest inscription, found out by him, is of Vikram Samvat (V.S.) 1112 and the latest is of V.S. 1987. In Vasishtashram, there are inscriptions of V.S. 1394 and V.S. 1506, relating to Kanhaddev, the son of Tej Singh of Chandravati and Rana Kumbha who donated some villages for benefit of this hermitage. In Achleshwar temple, the inscriptions are assignable to the times ranging, from the 13th to 18th century. A small figure of the goddess Mahis Mardini, is said to be of 8th century A.D. In Krodidhaja (Kotidhvaja) temple, there are inscriptions of V. S. 1204, on its two pillars. There are many other inscriptions and places of historical importance which have not come into limelight. They are to be deciphered and discovered. There is a plenty of further scope for research and exploration, in this field.

The earliest reference of 'Abu' or 'Arbuda' is found in the famous literary work 'Kuttani Matam' or Shambalimatam, written by Damodar Gupta (755-786 A.D.), the Chief Minister of Jayapida of Kashmir. In the Jain work 'Updeshasaptatika', there is a mention of ancient Jain Ācharya Pādalipta Suri (living in the 1st. Century A.D.) who used to fly daily to Abu along with other holy places of Shatrunjaya, Girnār, Ashtāpad and samet Shikar, for pilgrimage, by applying Lepa or ointment on his feet in accordance with Akāsh Gāmini Vidya (the Science of flying into the sky).[1] Before him also, came Svayamprabha Suri and Susthita Suri. Again Acharya Svayamprabha Suri, visited it, before his death which occured 52 years after Mahavir (i.e. 475 B.C.). He also instructed Raja Jai Sen of Shrimāl Nagar (modern Bhinmal) and made him his follower along with 90,000 families.[2] Acharya Susthita Suri, (the pupil of Arya Suhasti, the contemporary of Mauryan ruler Samprati) went on a pilgrimage to Ashtāpada from Arbudāchal and according to the Jain scriptures, he lived 291 years after Mahavir (i.e. 236 B.C.).[3] The references are also about the festivals or picnics which people enjoyed in Yātrā (pilgrimage to Prabhasa Pattan or at Mount Abbuya (Arbuda).[4] Acharya Deva Gupta Suri (IV) is said to have remained in meditation in Kandarā or cave of Abu when the four Goddesses Ambā, Padmā,

1. Updeshasaptatika 3-3.

2. Bhagwan Parashnath Ki Parampara Ka Itihas : Muni Gyan Sunderji, pp. 18-62.

3. Dhinipuri Tirtha Kalpa : Jinaprabhasuri (14th century A.D.).

4. Brhat Kalpa Bhāsya (composed in 6th Century A.D.) and edited by Muni Shri Puṇyavijayaji Vol. III 883-84.

Achyutā and Vijayā wanted to disturb him, but they could not swerve him from his path. These goddesses came over to Abu from Mahāvideha Ksetra (the holy place) after hearing the praise of the Suri from the living Jina (Viharmān) Sudharmā swami, that Deva Gupta was an unequalled celibate and also no one could surpass him in melody of his voice.[1]" Deva-Gupta Suri (IV) lived between 260 to 282 V.S. Later on, Acharya, Yakhasadev Suri (VI), stayed at Arbudāchal for sometime when he was visited by the goddesses Chakeshvari and Sachhāyikā and Deva Bhadra Sadhu of the order of Mahavir. He lived between 424 to 440 V.S.[2]. Shri Udyatan Suri, the pupil of Shri Vimalchandra Suri, the 33rd Pontiff from Mahavir, came on a pilgrimage to Abu in V.S. 994 (937-38 A.D.) These illustrations amply prove the very early existence of Jainism at Abu. An inscription of V.S. 1426 (1370 A.D.) was discovered by Muni Shri Jayantavijayaji from Mungthala (Mundasthala-Mahatirth), nearly 4 miles west from the foot of Mount Abu which refers about the visit of Lord Mahavir, in the Abu region when he toured as a monk, before attainment of perfect knowledge (Keval jnana).[3] This version, is further supported by another work Ashtottari—Tirthamala (verse 97), composed by Mahendra Suri (of Anchala-Gachha) in V.S. 1300 (243 A.D.) in which it is related that Mahavira had been to Arbuda Bhumi.

The great Jain ascetic Yogiraj Anand Ghanji (1606 to 1674 A.D.) used to practise Yoga (meditation), in the caves of Abu. He was found here, after great search, by another

1. Bhagvan Parashnath Ki Parampara Ka Itihas pp. 679.
2. Ibid. pp. 836.
3. From 'Arbudachala Pradakshinna Jain-Lekha Samdoh' Abu vol. v. pp. 17.

spiritual Guru Upadhyaya Yasho Vijayaji.[1] Very recently, Jagat Guru Acharya Vijaya Shanti Suriji, the king of ascetics and the greatest Yogiraja of the modern times, practised Yoga at Abu for a pretty long time and also breathed his last at Achalgarh (Abu).

General

Mount Abu is 17 miles and 6 furlongs from Abu Road Station, situated between Ahmedabad and Delhi, on the metre-gauge line, of the Western Railway. It is about 425 miles from Bombay, 115 miles from Ahmedabad and 275 miles from Jaipur. The route from Abu Road to Mount Abu, is metalled and coal-tarred. It is flat upto six miles and is crossed by Rajwār Banas Bridge, constructed in 1889 A.D. From Talehti, the ascent begins till we reach 'Chhipaberi Chowki'—the half-way house, between Abu Road and Mount Abu, covered with thick foliage of banyan trees. The slopes in the valley are covered with thick verdure which assumes a resplendent form after rains, while huge blocks of projecting dark-grey and purple rocks, contrasting with green trees and wild shrubs present a unique landscape-scenery. The clusters of bamboo trees, raise their heads high in the sky, amidst the thick shrubs, growing on the slopes. The journey is pleasant and the scenery all along the way is charming. As we approach nearer Mount Abu, the palm trees become visible, holding their umbrella-like heads, in the distant horizon. The air is cool, refreshing and sweet-scented. The regular buses of Rajasthan State Transport corporation, ply everyday, between Abu Road, to

1. Taken from the Gujarati book "Shri Anand Ghariji Nan Pado" written by Motichand Girdhari Lal Kapadiya and published by Shri Mahavir Jain Vidyalaya Govaliya, Tank, Bombay-2 published in 1956 A.D, pp. 34. The couplets of Anand Ghariji Maharaj, in mixed Hindi and Marwari, are as famous and popular as the songs of Meera, the strange coincidence being that both of them belonged to Merta.

Mount Abu and further to Delwada and Achalgarh. The distance from Mount Abu to Delwada, is 3 miles by bus route and 1½ miles by short route while the distance to Achalgarh is 4 miles from Delwada. The Municipal Board, Abu, levies the pilgrim tax from the pilgrims and visitors which is one rupee per head, from persons travelling by bus and Rupees two per head from tourists going by private Cars or Taxis. Along with the bus tickets, the tax tickets are purchased from the bus-stand at Abu Road which is just in front of Railway Station, Abu Road.

Abu, is specially crowded by a large number of pilgrims and visitors, during the summer season (April to June). During the autumn season (short season of September-October) also, a few people visit the hill. The visitors should take precautions against the chills, by wearing warm clothes when necessary. It is an excellent place, for convalescents, pleasure-seekers and meditators (yogis). This is also a big sanctuary for the students of history, archaeology, geography, geology, architecture, sculpture, botany, mountaineering and Indian medicines. The students of Gujarat and Rajasthan, mostly, come on their holiday-trips to the hill and carry with them immortal and indelible memories of this beautiful, celestial and historical mount.

THE DELWADA JAIN TEMPLES

Approach

On reaching Mount Abu, visitors are advised to make their own arrangements for their stay at Raghunathji Temple, Shanti-Sadan, hotels and lodges which are plenty in number. At Delwara, there are Svetamber and Digamber Jain Dharmashalas. The short route to Delwara is 1½ miles from Mount Abu and it passes by the Central Police Training College, Power House, Rajputana Club, Adhardevi and the Palace Hotel (Bikaner House). The State Teachers' Refresher Centre and the Tibetan Refugee School, are seen to the left and right side of the road. The view of the world-famous temples, can be had from the small bridge where the bus road meets. Then, ascending a few steps on the same road, we come to the tri-junction of roads to the south of which is a flight of steps, leading to the Digamber Jain Temple, on a high rock. A bye-path to the north, goes straight towards the famous Svetamber Jain Temples and we come to the north-east corner of Jain Svetamber Dharmashala, and reach a sloping and stony lane turning to the west and then passing by the main entrance of Jain Dharmashala, reach the temples by the southern gate, while the bye-path crosses over sloping ascent and ends before the Eastern gate of the Temples. Both the paths meet in a courtyard wherein is situated the office of Seth Kalyanji Parmannanji Sirohi—the managing trust of the temples. A sentry, in uniform, would be found always on duty, regulating the passengers, on the main gate of the temples. We reach the main gate by climbing seven foot-steps, from the court-yard. On the right of the main entrance, is seen a standing image of God Hanuman embossed on the wall. It is important to note that visitors are allowed to see the sculptures of the temples, between the fixed hours, i.e. 12 A.M. to 6 P.M. daily while for Jain worshippers, there is no such restriction. The Jains can enter the shrines for Darshan and Puja, till their doors are not closed. Shoes, belts and other articles of leather, arms, sticks and radios, are forbidden to be carried inside the temples. They are to be entrusted to the sentry on duty. Besides, visitors are not allowed to take the photos of the Jain idols enshrined in the temples.

Preliminary description

Before making entry into the temples, a preliminary description thereof, is worth-while. There are altogether five temples—four inside and one outside the main entrance. The temple of Mahavir Svami, Vimal-Vasahi, Luna-Vasahi, and Pitalhar are situated within one compound while the three-storeyed temple of Parashnath, known as Khartar-Vasahi, is seen towards south-east of the main entrance. Among all the temples, Vimal-Vasahi and Luna-Vasahi are most notable. Abu, is famous, all over the world on account of these two superb Jain shrines at Delwada. Vimal Vasahi was built by Vimal Shah, the minister and Commandar-in-Chief of Bhimdev I, the king of Gujarat, in 1031 A.D. and Luna-Vasahi, was constructed later, in 1231 A.D.. by Vastupal and Tej Pal, both brother ministers of the King Viradhaval, of Gujarat. Luna Vasahi, was named after Luna-Singh, the son of Tej Pal.

"The Delwara temples are among the oldest Shrines standing almost unrivalled as masterpieces of architecture and sculpture. In spite of ill-usage and poor restoration, they retain a bewildering wealth of perhaps the finest marble-carving in India. They find a filling framework in a nest of mango groves and green fields of barley waving at their feet and high hills, surrounding them on all sides." The plan in both the temples, consists of a shrine, a porch and an arcade court-yard with niches for images. All the pillars and images are of delicately carved white marble. The characteristic of the design is streamlined grace and lightness with decorative carving embracing the whole interior executed with great elaboration and detail. The ceilings of the porticoes are richly carved, illustrating many scenes from Jain and Hindu Scriptures while the domes in the centre of two temples are most striking. In the main shrines, niches and the cells around the courtyard are seated the images of Jain Tirthankars in silent, stoic, staring and meditating poses, at the sight of whom, the pilgrims find great solace. from the worldly hum-drum of life on the plains below.

The Temple of Mahavir Svami

Now, we pass through the main entrance of the temples and see the clusters of shrines, interspersed with the luxuriant mango and Champak trees. Turning to the left of the doorway, we find the temple of Mahavir Svami or the Lord Mahavir—the twenty-fourth and the last Tirthankar of the present age. It consists of small shrine, a closed hall opened to the north and a porch in front of the temple. It might have been built 200 or 300 years ago. The paintings on the ceilings and the walls, inside the hall, are in dark red colour, painted by the artists of Sirohi in V.S. 1821 (1764 A.D.). The names of the artists and the year with date and month have been written, on the upper wall to the left side. The flowers, pigeons, court-scenes, dancing girls, horses and elephants and other scenes, have been painted nicely. In the shrine on each side of the idol of Mahavir, there are three Jain idols of different Tirthankers, i.e. six small idols in all. On the left side of the hall, outside the shrine, there is a big Patta or marble slab of rectangular size with a triangular-shaped stone over it, containing 133 miniature-sized Jain images with a small Jain image in the centre.

From the painted words and figures, as well as from the year of composition of 'Hirsaubhagya Maha Kavya', (V.S. 1639) in which there is no mention of this temple, it can be inferred that this temple was constructed after V.S. 1639 (1582 A.D.) and before V.S. 1821 (1764 A.D.). The definite date and year of its Pratishta or consecration ceremony, have not come to light. There are no decorated carvings in the interior of the shrine as well as outside it. The pillars and the floor of the hall are simple in design.

Vimal Vasahi

From the porch of Mahavir Svami temple, we enter Mukha-Mandap or portico to the west of which is an entrance to Vimal Vasahi. Stepping on the conch-designed pedastal, we pass through the principal door and come down to the open corridor, on raised platform running on all sides of the court-yard of the temple. There are 59 Devakulikas or small shrines, each facing the main shrine of Lord Rikhabdev or Shri Ādīshavar, the first of Jain Tirthankars. The array of 52 cells or small shrines, is common in all the Jain temples of Bavanjinalaya. In this temple, seven additional cells are found, among them one is the cell of Ambaji, the tutelary goddess of the temple and the other two are of Lord Munisuvrat, the twentieth Tirthankar.[1] These cells are old and adjacent to them four new cells have been erected and six renovated during the total repairs of the temples done by Seth

1. Some regard it as the idol of Lold Rikhabdev. Being a very old idol, it could not be identified correctly.

Anandji Kalyanji, Pedhi, Ahmedabad, the representative institution of Jain Svetambar community of India, done at the cost of Rs. 13,82,751, from V.S. 2007 to V.S. 2019 at the hands of the Architect Shri Amrit Lal Mool Chand Trivedi of Sompura.[1]

Corridors

A visitor, at the first sight, would be bewildered to look at the richly carved corridors, pillars, arches, mandaps or porticoes and he would be in a fix as to which direction, he should move first. The writer would prefer to take him, first to the left of the principal door, facing the main sanctum, in the corridors. There are double corridors on all sides of the court-yard, except on the west. The pillars supporting the ceilings of the corridors, are simple in design but they are all arrayed in two equal lines which look beautiful, from distance. On the ceilings are engraved different kinds of rich and elaborate designs of lotus-buds, petals and flowers, geometrical figures, the miniature-sized Jain images and the scenes of Jain and Hindu mythological tales. In front of each cell, on the marble floor, is slightly raised pedestal, almost semi-circular in shape and having on each side, a conch carved out. It is called 'Sankhāvali' or 'an array of conches'. On the outerwalls of the cells, near the entrance, are seen Jain shrāvakas and shrāvikas—Jain laymen and laywomen with folded hands, bands of elephants, ducks and lotus-buds.

We begin from the passage in the corridor which leads to Rangmandap. The first ceiling of the passage adjacent to the door, depicts an Acharya, (Monk) sitting on simhasan (throne-like seat), with sthāpana (a kind of wooden

1. The inscription of V.S. 2019 Margshirsh Shukla 1, Wednesday has been incised on the outer wall of cell no. 18.

holder for putting rosary etc.) and Jain laymen or Shravakas hearing his discourse while the second domical ceiling shows a row of elephants in the lower panel and the scene of Ardrakumar imparting, right knowledge to an elephant is depicted in the upper panel.[1] The elephant, is seen in the centre, bowing to the Jain monk (Ardrakumar), behind whom are two more Jain monks. At the end of this panel, Mahavir, stands in meditation. On the other side of the elephant, a man is seen fighting with a lion. In front of cells no, 2 and 3, on the walls of their doors, are seen relief carvings of Jain laymen and laywomen holding offerings for worship. The similar carvings, are found depicted in front of cells No. 11, 29 (old No. 24), 31(26), 43(38), 44 (39), 45(40), 47(42), 48(43), 49(44), 57(52), 58 (53), and 59 (54). In front of cell No. 7, one of the beams of the second bay, is divided into three panels-lowermost showing a row of ornamental lotus-buds, the middle one depicting a row of diamonds while the uppermost representing some human figures. The first ceiling, in front of

1. The story of Ardrakumar is long and interesting one. In brief, it is said that Ardrakumar, was the son of a king named Ārdraka, ruling over non-Aryan country. He contracted friendship with Abhayakumar, the son of king Shrenik (Bimbsar—6th Century B.C.) who sent an image of Jina, at the sight of which he gained the knowledge of his past life. He renounced the world and became a Jain monk. Once, when he was proceeding to Lord Mahavir, as a monk, he came across 500 robbers who turned as Sadhus, on his instruction. Later on, he saw a hermitage of Tāpasas or ascetics known as Hasti-tapasa-ashrama where an elephant was tied to a post nearby to be killed because the inmates of the Ashram believed that in eating various fruits there was a greater sin than in killing an elephant which would last for a number of days and would involve only one life. The elephant ran amok, approached Ardrakumar and gently touched his feet with his trunk, after bending his front legs. The Muni Ardrakumar instructed him in the path of true religion and so also the Tapasas who became Jain sadhus later on.

cell No. 8, shows a Samavasarana[1] of a Jina, with chomukh. The second and the third circular bands, round the samavasarana, show a person on simhāsan, some other men, elephants and horses, close to the second ceiling, in front of cell No. 8, one of the beams shows an adoration of Jain monk by three of his pupils and three Jain Laymen and the other beam depicts two monks and their disciple as well as two Shravakas standing with folded hands. A mad elephant is also seen running after some people who are being scared away.

In the first ceiling, of cell No. 9, are depicted five Kalyanaks (chief auspicious events in the life of Jina which are stated below :—1. Chayavan-Kalyanak or the ceremony observed when Jina comes into the womb of his mother 2. Janma—Kalyanak or the birth ceremony 3. Diksā-Kalyānak or Renunciation ceremony 4. Jnana Kalyanak or ceremony when Jina obtains keval Jnāna (perfect knowledge) and 5. Nirvana Kalyanak or ceremony when Jina leaves his mortal body and obtains final liberation.

In front of cell No. 10, first ceiling contains the scenes from the life of Neminath. The central circle represents a tank full of water wherein are seen sporting Krishna, his queens and Neminath. The second circular band, shows Neminath, blowing the conch in the armoury of Krishna and the trial of strength between the two, while the third band depicts king Ugrasen, his daughter princess Rajimati, the marriage Pandāl, cattle-shed, Nemi's marriage procession, his turning back, Diksa procession, the initia-

1. Samavasarana, is a kind of circular designed audience hall in which the Jina, after attaining perfect knowledge (Keval jnana) delivers his sermon, facing the East and his voice is heard by men, elephants, horses and other animals who sit in three circular bands below the Jina, and hear his speech, in their own language though he speaks in one language.

tion and the scene of attainment of Keval jnāna (perfect knowledge). On the outer wall of this cell No. 10, to the right of entrance are incised, 120 dates of all Kalyānaks of 24 Tirthankars, according to the five Kalyanaks or chief events of each Tirthankar as mentioned above.

Cell No. 11, first ceiling illustrates a fine sculpture of goddess with fourteen hands and the cow is shown as her vehicle. She may be identified as Mahā-Rohini or Multi-armed variety of the first Jain Vidyadevi or the goddess of knowledge.

Cell No. 12, first ceiling represents the five Kalyānaks of Lord Shantinath—the sixteenth Tirthankar, including the scene from his previous existence, as king Megh-ratha who cut the flesh of his body and weighed it equal to the weight of a pigeon who came for shelter against the chasing falcon. This bird was no other than god Sarupa who came on the earth, to deviate the king, from his path of Dharma. This god, in the form of pigeon, began to increase his weight by his supernatural power, but the king remained steadfast to his promise and was pre red to sacrifice himself, in order to protect the pigeon.

The newly constructed ten cells from No. 18 to No. 27, perfectly resemble the old cells, in design and details. None can distinguish them from the others. The best specimen is the image of Shankeshvari Devi, in front of cell No. 20, second row. In the south-western corner, behind the two new cells No. 23 and 24, there is a big hall containing a huge black sculpture of Munisuvrata (Rikhabdev ?) According to the legend, Brahamins of the place surrounding the temple area, demanded a cogent proof of the existence of any trace of Jainism, from Vimal Shah. The minister Vimal fasted for three days propitiating the goddess Amba who appeared in a dream and showed to him, the spot (inside the hall) from where came out the Jain image of about 2460 years (of fourth Āra or fourth sub-Division of Avasarpini age, according to the Jain texts), on digging out the ground near the champak tree and Svastik of Kankum (vermilion colour). This fact satisfied the local Brahmins before whom the place was dug out. Then Vimal Shah, installed this very idol, at this very place, in the year V.S. 1088 (1031 A.D.) and later on installed a very beautiful brass image of Rikhabdev as the Mula-nayak (main deity), in the main sanctum. In the hall, we find many other Jain idols and other sculptures, out of which three of them are important to mention. The first is Samavasaran or circular construction as mentioned before, on the uppermost division of which is seated the Tirthankar, whose face is seen on all the four sides, delivering the sermon, to the gods and goddesses, monks and nuns, laymen and laywomen, animals and birds etc. They are all seen assembled, in three different circular sections, forming his audience or Parkhdā. The second Sculpture is of Shri Hira Vijaya Suri, the preceptor of the Moghul Emperor Akbar, in front of the famous idol of Muni Suvrat Svami, This statue of renowned Jain Acharya, was installed by Mahāmahopādhyaya Shri Labdhi Sagar Suri in V.S. 1661 (1604 A.D.), according to the inscription on pedestal. By the side of it, are seen the portrait sculptures of two pairs of shravakas and shravikas, holding garlands, in their hands. The third figure, adjacent to the main deity, on the north-western corner, is that of Valināh, in standing posture. Valinah—the spirit of the locality used to obstruct, the minister Vimalshah, in the construction of the temple. But the brave minister, conquered him in a duel, carrying a sword in his hand when the offering or boiled corn and sweets could not satisfy the spirit who demanded flesh and wine which the minister declined to offer, in accordance with the principles of his religion. From the hall, a narrow passage, on the eastern side, leads to a long inner apartment which is divided into two, by an open door. In these two apartments, are arranged the images of Jinas, in two rows.

Next to the cells No. 23 and 24, we come to cell No. 25 in which is enshrined the beautiful image of goddess Amba who appeared before Vimal Shah in a dream and helped him from time to time, in the construction of this famous temple. There are three other small-sized images of the goddess. The main image is impressive with bold carving. She bears the miniature image of Jina on her head.

A beautiful representative of Krishna, subduing the Kalia snake, is seen in the ceiling of cell No. 34 (old No. 29). There are two different versions in Jain and Hindu texts. According to Jains, Krishna subdued Kalia-snake, by dragging him out of the water and kept him alive on the request of his seven queens. This event took place when Krishna was on his way to kill Kansa, to take revenge of his six brothers who were killed by Kansa, on the words of Atimuktaka Muni which were told to his wife that the seventh issue born of the marriage pair-Vasudeva and Devaki would be the destroyer of her husband. Krishna was the seventh issue of this marriage pair. Krishna, killed Kansa, ultimately. The Hindu version is that Krishna and his friends were playing with a ball. When it fell into the river, Yamunā, Krishna jumped into the waters to fetch it. At that time Kaliā-Nāg (Snake) obstructed him, but he subdued it, with his superior power.

In the second ceiling, in front of cell No. 40. (35), there is a representation of a goddess, sitting on lion vehicle and being attended by two six-armed males standing by her sides. She is supposed to be Jain Vidyadevi-Mahamansi. She carries several symbols in her sixteen hands.

The second ceiling of cell No. 44 (39), depicts a unique carving of four goddesses, with a lotus flower in the middle.

They are said to be the images of Sarasvati, Lakshmi, Shakti and Kalika on each of the corner of the ceiling, with their vehicles of the swan, elephant, lotus and demon repectively. The second ceiling of cell No. 45 (40), represents the goddess Lakshmi, surrounded by eight Dikpalas or guardians of quarters. On the side of the beam enclosing it, the figures of standing Tirthankaras have been carved. Further, on the two side panels of the second ceiling, in front of cell No. 47(42), are seen carved beautiful figures of Lakshmi or the goddess of wealth.

In front of cells No. 48(43) 49(44) and 50(45), each of the second bay contains respectively Vajrashrinkla, (one of sixteen Jain goddessess of knowledge) carrying a chain and riding on a horse vehicle, Sarasvati (the goddess of learning) riding on a swan and Vairatya (the Jain goddess of knowledge) with a cobra as her vehicle.

On the beams of the first ceiling of cell No. 51(46), are the figures of standing Jinas and Shravakas carrying garlands for worship while the second ceiling shows a remarkable relief of many-armed Nrsimha (Man-lion) tearing as under the belly of Hiranya-Kashyapa, caught between his legs.[1]

The first ceiling of cell No. 52(47) represents the

1. According to Hindu mythology, the demon Hiranya-Kashyapa, had obtained a boon from Brahma (the creator of the Universe) that he would neither be killed by gods, demons, human-beings or animals nor would he die inside or outside a structure, neither in the day nor at night; neither with any weapon nor with any instrument, neither on earth nor in the sky and so on. Obviously, he wanted to eliminate the chances of death. The demon had a pious son named Prahalād—a great devotee of Vishnu. The father tortured him, for his being true worshipper of god. The god Vishnu, ultimately rescued his devotee and killed the demon without disturbing the boon granted by Brahma, by assuming a half-human, Man-lion form and killed him on the doorstep of the palace, at the time of twilight, holding him tight between his legs (thus above the ground and not in sky), tearing his belly with sharp lion-finger nails.

the birth-rites of a Jina, being performed by fifty-six Dik-Kumaris or quarter-maidens, carrying water-jars, incense-bearers, fans, mirrors etc. The second ceiling of cell No. 53 (48) is divided into twenty small sections representing small relief carvings of Tirthankars, Acharyas and his pupils. The first ceiling of cell No. 54 (49) depicts nearly the similar carving. The first ceiling of cell No. 58(53), has the carvings of a Jina in meditating pose with Shravakas standing beside him and an Acharyas with a Sthapana, in front and Shravakas standing with folded hands.

In front of the last cell No. 59 (54), the first ceiling contains a row of elephants and a Jina, standing in meditating posture, attended by Jain worshippers carrying jars, flowers, garlands and other articles of worship.

This finishes the important description of the ceiling and the portions of the outerwalls of the cells, in the corridor or Bhamati of Vimal Vasahi.

Courtyard

After taking the complete round, we come again to the main passage which leads to Rangmandap. From here, we step down on the courtyard 98 feet in length and 42 feet in breadth. The structure, in the courtyard, consisting of the main shrine with its Gudhamandap and other mandaps, is cruci-form in plan.

Between the passage platform and Rangmandap, there is an open big porch, having three ceilings, the central of which represents the fight between Bharat and Bahubali, the two sons of Lord Rikhab Dev the first Tirthankara and the attainment of Kevaljnana or supreme knowledge by Bharat. In this scene, are depicted the city of Ayodhya with Bharat's sisters, queens, chariots, rows of elephants, horses and infantry, on one side and the city of Takhsa Shila, on the other side, with similar representations of

Bahubali, his minister, harem and army. The third relief is of the battlefield and the next two panels indicate the six types of duels between Bharat and Bāhubali, namely Drishti-Yuddha (gazing contest), Vāk-Yuddha (contest in dialogues) Bāhu-Yuddha (hand-to-hand fight), Mushti-Yuddha (boxing), Danda-Yuddha (duel of fight with a staff in hand), Chakra-Yuddha (fight with disc weapon). The fifth relief shows the figure of Bahubali in meditation, with creepers entwining his legs and ant-hills growing round him. In one corner, is seen the representation of Samavasarana or congregation of Lord Rishbha and the last relief represents the attainment of Kevaljñana, by Bharat, after his renunciation of the World, on looking at his ringless finger. A goddess, is also shown, giving him the accessories of a Jain monk, namely Rajoharan (a broom of woolen strings with a wooden handle at the end.)[1]

On either side of the central ceiling of the portico, there are exuberant carvings of bunches of flowers and of dancing figures in the domed ceilings, unsurpassed by any other corridor ceilings.

1. The story in short runs like this :—The first Tirthankar Rishabha had 100 sons and two daughters namely Brāhmi and Sundri. Rikabdev when he was a king, divided his kingdom among his sons. Bharat was the crowned king of Ayodhyā and Bahubali of Takhsa-shila and so on. Bharat started on World-conquest. All his brothers except Bahubali, accepted his sovereignty. Bharat, had, therefore, to challenge his brother Bahubali. But in order to avoid large-scale bloodshed, they entered into six kinds of duels, to decide the battle. In all duels, except the last, Bahubali, was the winner. In the last duel of disc-weapon, Bharat used Chakra-ratna against the accepted principles and this fact aroused disgust in Bahubali's mind against the World. On the very battlefield, he plucked off the hair of his head, from the very fist which was raised against his brother and became a monk, practising such rigorous austerities for one complete year till ant-hills grew round him and creepers spread over his limbs but he did not obtain the Kevaljnana. Then, as he prepared himself to start for paying respects to his brother monks who had already got Kevalajnana; at the suggestion of his two sisters that he should shake off his pride and egoism, he attained Kevalajnana.

Rangmandap

From the portico, we come to Rangamandap—a big open and spacious hall, meant specially for dancing, music and festivals. This is slightly raised from the level of the courtyard. "This open pavilion, is composed of a central nave based on an octagonal plan, with eight pillars, supporting the dome of the nave. In front and to the north and south of this mandap, are attached three open porticoes resting on ornamental pillars with their separate domes or ceilings. The Rangamandap is a separate structure altogether, supported by its rectangular ceiling which itself is supported by a row of four extra-pillars, on each side, the ceiling being divided into three sections or bays. The porticoes to the north and south of Rangmandap extend beyond the line of transcepts of the Gudhamandap and almost fill up the space of the open courtyard. It seems that Prithvi Pal, the descendant of Vimal Shah adorned the shrine with a mandap and repaired the temple in 1206 V.S. (1149-50) A.D.

About the marvellous beauty of the pillars and the dome over Rangmandap, the Government of India Publication Says :—

'The richness of marvellously carved and figured columns of the Vimal Vasahi, the wealth of delicate carving in the dome, made up of eleven concentric rings containing patterns of human figures and animals, elephant processions, repetitions of images in niches and endless dancing figures take our breath away. Between these figure courses are ornamental repeats which towards the apex culminate in a group of pendants. Supporting these circular rings is a series of sixteen brackets, tho figures of the goddesses of knowledge (Vidya Devis)". Between the Rangmandap and the corridor, there are two porticoes attached to the mandap on two sides. On the northern side is a sculpture of Sarasvati, and on the southern side is carved in the centre a beautiful lotus, and a charming figure of Lakshmi. On the four corners of Rangamandap, there are figures of gods and goddesses out of which only the beautiful figure of the goddess Ambika is legible.

Nochowki

A main entrance to the sanctum, is in the middle of the wall of the Gudhmandap covering the western side of Nochowki. Nochowki, is divided into nine sections by ornamental pillars, having nine ceilings of different sculptures, the prominent being the representations of Tirthankar in meditation, and an Acharya with his disciple, in the central dome, the figure of goddess Lakshmi being lustrated by elephants, and the fight of two elephants as shown on the right hand side corners and the scene of sea-foam is seen in the central ceiling, on the left hand side. It resembles the ceiling of Shaik Farid Tomb and of the Vimal Vasahi temple on the Shatrunjaya hill. In the rest of the ceilings, lotus flowers and other fine figures have been depicted. Nochowki is used mostly for ritual worships or Pujas.

Gudhamadap

Now, we enter the door of Gudhamandap or canopied hall in front of the main sanctury of the principal deity—Lord Rikhabdev. On the outer walls of both sides of the entrance, there are reliefs of Jinas, Jain monks and nuns with Jain laymen and Laywomen, bending down to pay respects to them. In Gudhamandap, there are two prominent standing idols of Lord Parashvanath in meditative postures. They are better known as "Kausagayas" in Jain Shastras. Opposite to these figures on the inner wall of the entrance, are placed two images of laymen and three of laywomen, with Naulis and Thelis (old-fashioned money-bags), representing the relatives of Vijada who carried out repairs in V.S. 1378. These fine portrait sculptures are important for the study of dress and ornaments of Gujarat in the fourteenth century. The males kept beards and moustaches and wore dhotis upto knees while the females wore saris upto ankles and their bodice left the part of the belly bare. To the north and south of this hall, there are two big entrance doors with strong wooden doorways which lead to two open porticoes or transcepts which are quite a few steps from the level of the courtyard. The porticoes have also ornate door-frames and their pillars too, are adorned with the reliefs of gods and goddesses. The Gudhamandap is meant for Chaitya-Vandan or obeisance and Arti or waving of the lamps, before the Mulnayak or the principal deity.

As we step towards the principal idol of the main sanctum, we see on both sides of the walls, two images of Jinas seated in two niches. Nobody is permitted to enter the main temple except those Jain laymen and laywomen, who take their bath and wear Puja Clothes, for Puja (Worship). In the interior of the sanctum, there is a big and beautiful white idol of the First Tirthankar, Lord Rikhabdev or Ādīshvar Bhagvan, set in finely sculptured Parikar or paraphernalia with attended figures etc. around, including figures of four other Jinas. This whole image with Parikar, is known as Saparikar Panchtirthi of Rikhabdeva. Every morning and every evening after sunset, auction is held by the Pujāri or Bhojak. (the master of ceremonies) for the first Puja and first Ārti waving of lamps, in terms of maunds of ghee, with an open bid of half a maund. The bidder of one maund of ghee, has to pay rupees two and a half. According to this rate, the highest bidder has to deposit the money in the office of the temples. The amount thus collected, is utilised for meeting the cost of saffron, flowers, incense and allied articles relating to the worship of the Jain idol. The highest bidder, has the right to perform the Puja or Arati, first of all, among the worshippers present in the shrine. This practice is prevalent, in almost all the Jain Tirthas or Jain temples which are considered as the places of pilgrimage, though the rate of the bid of ghee might vary. The Jain laymen and laywomen, consider themselves very fortunate, for getting the first chance of performing the Puja or Arati, at a place of pilgrimage. They deem it as a pious act.

The Shikhar or sanctuary of the main shrine and the attending small shrines are small in contrast to the sanctuaries of the temples at Khajurāho, Bhuvaneshwar and other lofty temples in India. From the distance, it hardly appears as a temple. Moreover, there are no carvings in the exterior of the temples and also in the main shrine and Gudhamandap. The reasons for these disparities, are not far to seek. In V.S. 1368 (1311 A.D.) the muslim invaders, destroyed both the temples at Delwada (Vimal Vasahi and Luna Vasahi). The demolition has been so extensive and thorough that almost all the sanctuaries, the gudhamandaps and almost all the images of Tirthankars might have been broken to pieces and in their place, the interiors of sanctum and gudhamandaps might have been rebuilt and therefore, in later repairs, there are no exterior ornamentations. Prithvi Pal, the descendant of Vimal Shah repaired the shrine in 1206 V.S. It is uncertain whether the shrine needed repairs due to faulty construction or because it suffered spoilation at the hands of fanatic invader like Allaudin Khilji who invaded Jālor fort, north-west of Abu in V.S. 1368 and captured it. It is just possible that he might have attacked Abu and destroyed these shrines while returning from Jalor.

This shrine was constructed by Vimal Shah, after many trials and tribulations. He was a great commander and minister of the king Bhim Dev I of Gujarat. He showed high gallantry and heroism on the battle-grounds and defeated Hamir Sumro of Sindh and subdued the king of Chedi and also Dhandhuk of Chandrāvati, near Abu. He also demonstrated great strength, courage and fearlessness, in encounters with a lion aud a wrestler, arranged by the king Bhimdeva, at the instance of his jealous ministers. He was so proficient in archery that he, with his closed eyes, could shoot down the bird sitting on a tree and could pierce through anyone of eight betal-leaves, put together, on the stomach of a lying child, by the aim of his arrow. He could touch the moving ear-rings of a young lady, while churning curd, by the mark of his arrow. He remained the governor of Chandravati, after taking it from Dhundhuk and made it a prosperous city. Once, the famous monk Acharya Dharma Ghosh Suri came at Chandrāvati and he was so much influenced by his sermons that he asked for the atonement of the past sinful acts committed by him in the battlefield. The Acharya suggested him for renovation of ancient Abu Jain Tirth. By the construction of a Jain shrine at Abu, he would be wiping out his own sins along with those of the pilgrims visiting this holy place. He performed a great wonder on the surface of the earth, by erecting shrine, for attainment of the path of peace and perfection for the soul.

This artistic performance was accomplished by a renowned architect of a village near Badnagar in Gujarat, by the name of Kīrtidhar. He belonged to that class of artisans who built great fortresses in the South. This architect had lost his wife and a young son and was naturally disgusted with the world. He first declined to build the shrine but later on, looking at the sincerity and genorosity of Vimal Shah, he agreed to build such a wonderful temple which would spread the fame of the minister far and wide. The shrine was completed, after hard labour of 1500 masons and 1200 labourers during the period of fourteen years. The marble stones were brought from the mines in the Arasoor hill, near Ambaji, on the backs of elephants.

Vimal had to pass through many ordeals before the completion of the temple. First of all, the minister fasted for three continuous days to propitiate the goddess Ambaji for two boons—one for the birth of a son and the other for construction of an ideal temple at Abu. The goddess being pleased, could only grant one of the two boons and she left the choice to Vimal, who selected the latter boon on sanguine advice of his prudent wife Shridattā. The boon being granted, Vimal had to seek permission for the land at Abu, from his master, King Bhimdeva. Although permission was given by the king but the Brahmins or Joshis as they were called, put obstacles in his way, by claiming the land as their own. The pious minister, did not exercise his state influence, in ecclesiastical matter like this and pacified the Brahmins, by offering them special rectangular shaped gold Mohurs, spread over the entire land covered by the temple area. The purpose behind minting the rectangular pieces of gold, was that no space was left out between one piece and another and so spread over the ground, the owners of land would be fully compensated. The case would have been different, if round gold mohurs were placed.

As the work bagan to commence, there was another hurdle from the spirit Valinah—Kshetra Pāl deity—who used to dismantle the day's work at night by his supernatural power. Vimal, tried to appease the spirit, by offering him boiled corn and sweets but he demanded flesh and wine which was totally denied by the minister, being a true Jain. He fought bravely with the spirit, taking sword in his hand and conquered the spirit. All kinds of obstacles, being removed, the work began to proceed swiftly and it was completed within short space of time, by providing special facilities to the masons and labourers who had to work in the bitter and cold days on the mountain, specially in the winter. It is said that Vimal installed the brass image of Lord Rikhabdev, of 57 inches in height and 18 bharas in weight but no trace is found of this idol. The present marble image was installed in later years. This finishes the description of Vimal Vasahi, the most artistic and highly religious place of the world.

Hasti-Shala of Vimal Vasahi

After seeing Vimal Vasahi., we make our exit from the principal door from which we entered and step down in a big porch, to the east of which is Hasti-Shālā or the Hall of Elephants of Vimal Shah, which is a big roofed hall with latticed walls containing figures of almost geometrical designs. As said above, it was built, at the time of the repairs, in the year V.S. 1204, by the minister Prithvi Pāl, a descendant in the fourth line of the minister Nedha, the elder brother of Vimal Shah. Just opposite to the doorway, we see an equestrian figure of the minister and general Vimal Shah, wearing a crown, holding a dish and a cup in his right hand and controlling the big horse with his left hand. Behind him, is seated an attendant keeping chattra or an umbrella over his head. In the hall are the marble sculptures of elephants, arrayed in rows, beautifully carved, well-modelled and adorned with seats (howdas), trappings etc., two of them carrying a Mahavat and a minister, on their backs. On one, there is left only a Sheth or one of the ancestors of Vimal and three elephants have figurers of riders alone while no figures are found on four elephants. Behind the row of elephants a representation of Samavasarana, circular in shape with three fortifications and on the top there is four-faced miniature image of Jina. The inscription of 1292 V.S. on it shows that it was built by one Dhāndhuka Oswal by caste and the follower of a Nanna-acharya of Koranta gaccha. The figures of seven elephants were built by Prithvi Pal in 1204 V.S. The figure of second elephant behind samavasarana and the two elephants in the last row, were erected by Dhanpal, the elder son of Prithvi Pal, in V.S. 1277. On the outer wall of Hasti-Shala, facing the east, are carved out 16 Jina figures on pilasters of the wall section which has a window in it, while on the arch above the pilasters are carved 76 more Jina figures making 92 in all, out of which 72 are the Jain Tirthankars of past, present and future ages (twenty-four of each age) and the rest 20 are the idols of Viharaman (living) Jinas of the present age. On the inner face of the arch are seen 70 miniature figures of Tirthankars and two more on the side pillars, totalling to 72 which represent three chovisis.

Returning from Hasti-Shala, we come to the porch again which might have been constructed between V.S. 1639 and V.S. 1821. This was not existing when Acharya Hirvijaya Suri, paid a visit to this shrine in 1639 V.S., as could be inferred from Hira-saubhagya Mahakavya, referring to his visit. Under the porch, in front of Hasti-Shala, are Surahis (Sanskrit surbhi or cow) on which cows are carved out and below them, were inscribed words forbidding collection of any kind of taxes from worshippers or pilgrims of the temples of Vimal Vasahi and Luna-Vasahi. These inscriptions were got prepared in

V.S. 1372, 1373 and 1377, by Chauhan Māhāraval Lumbāji, the ancestor of the last ruler of erstwhile Sirohi State. On a small pillar in the porch, are the two figures of the same person, the first figure riding on the horse and the second one with folded arms, both being attended by an umbrella-bearer. His wife and son, are standing near his side. The inscription on it, ascribes one Sobhita, the brother of famous Jain poet Shripal of Chaulukya court of Patan who lived in the 12th Century of Vikram era.

Then, we find the portrait figures of Thākkura Āmpasā (Ambā prasād) and Tha Śitadevi, parents of Kavardi or Kaparddin the famous minister-in-chief (Mahamatya) of the king Kumar Pal, standing with folded hands in adoration of the Lord, on the left hand side of Hasti-Shala, by the side of the pillar. The minister was a pious, rich, generous, valiant and learned. He was killed, in boiling oil, under a trap laid down by Ajaya Pāl (the successor of Kumar Pal), who had malign and hatred towards Jainism. This slab of stone was installed by Acharya Shri Dharma Ghosh Suri in V.S. 1226 as evinced by the inscription on it.

LUNA-VASAHI

Introductory

From the porch, in front of Hasti-Shala of Vimal Shah, we turn to the north, after passing by an open doorway and ascending the flight of steps, we find ourselves on an open platform to the left of which is a Digamber Jain Temple of Lord Kunthu Nath, the seventeenth Tirthankar. A way higher up, to the left of the temple, goes to the quarters of the Pujaris or paid worshippers of the Śvetamber temple. In front of the Digamber Jain temple, towards the north-east, on the open platform, we see another important temple, known as 'Luna-Vasahi', built by Vastupal Tej Pal, the ministers of Gujarat, in 1230 A.D., 200 years after the construction of Vimal Vasahi. This famous temple was named after Luna Singh, the son of the minister Tejpal, at the cost of Rs. 12,53,00,000 for the spiritual benefit of Luna Singh and Anupmadevi—the wife of Tejpal. These two brothers, were brave, pious and generous. They were also liberal in their outlook and bore no hatred or animosity against any religion. They spent crores of rupees not only for constructing the Jain temples and Upāsaras (residences for Jain monks) but also for Hindu shrines, mosques, water-sheds, wells, tanks, free alm-houses, rest-houses embankments, bridges and other works of public importance for the general welfare. They had broad vision and great tolerance. In Mahāmātya Vastupal, there was a harmonious combination of wealth and learning which is rarely found. He was a great scholar and the contemporary poets called him 'Dharmaputra of Sarasvati' (the son of the goddess of learning).

No one could surpass these two brothers, in their charity and generosity. in the Jain World. They spent enormous amount in the repairs of Shatrunjaya and Girnar Jain Tirthas and for writing down the ancient Jain texts. A long list can be prepared of the various works, of these two brothers.

Design and pattern

The permission was sought from the king Bhimdev II of Gujarat and Som Singh, the feudatory Parmar Chief of Abu, for building Luna-Vasahi. The design and pattern of Luna Vasahi was adopted from Vimala Vasahi which was built earlier. "Like Vimal Vasahi, Luna Vasahi is an example of fine chiselling of marble. The walls, doors, pillars, mandaps, ceilings or domes etc. are adorned with ornamental relief carvings of inanimate motifs like flowers, trees, creepers, lamps, bells etc., or of animals like horses, elephants, camels, tigers and lions or of fishes and birds, various representations of gods and men, of scenes from life such as courts, royal processions, marriage scenes, dramas, music parties, battle scenes, grazing animals, voyages by sea, life of shepherds, rites of monks and Jain laymen and women and scenes from the lives of Tirthankars or other great men of Jain mythology."

It is difficult to compare the two temples and to remark as to which is superior to the other. "Vimal Vasahi is superior in one respect at least and that is especially from human life, as also from the richness of carvings over almost all its component parts. The Luna-Vasahi, however excels in style and beauty of carvings, as for example, in the relief panels from the life of Krishna or in the group of female dancers and musicians." One special feature of Luna-Vasahi is said to be the two niches or Gokhs of Derāni (wife of the younger brother) and Jethāni (wife of the elder brother), the wives of Tej Pal and Vastupal, built at the cost of 18 lacs of rupees for building both the niches. They have excellent ornamental carvings which obtain admiration from all visitors. This popular belief is not supported by historical record which tells that they were built by the minister Tejpal, for the spiritual benefit of his second wife Suhadādevī, according to the inscriptions on both the niches. They were consecrated in V.S. 1297.

The architect of the shrine was Shobhandev, a skilled artist of his times, belonging to Gujarat. There were 48 cells round the main shrine of Lord Neminath, the 22nd Tirthankar of Jains. But, during the repairs between V.S. 2007 and V.S. 2019, 4 cells have been added making the total 52 and 4 cells were renovated. Thus the cells Nos. 23 to 30, have been newly built in the corridor by Anandji Kalyanji Pedhi, Ahmedabad. The Pratishthā or consecration ceremony of the main temple was performed on Sunday, the 3rd day of dark half of the month of Chaitra 1287 V.S. (1230 A.D) with great pomp and show, by Acharya Vijaisen Suri of Nagendra gaccha. The cells were consecrated during the years 1287 V.S. and 1293 V.S., while the Pratishthā of two Gokhs (niches) were held in V.S. 1297 (1240 A.D.). The minister Tejpal established a trust for the management and protection of the shrine and also for the expenses of the festivals and worship, on different holy days in every year. The builders of the temple, declared this trust, sitting before the Lord, in the Rangamandap of Luna-Vasahi and in the presence of Somsingh, the ruler of Chandrāvati along with his prince Kānhad (Krishna) and others before Guguli Brahamins, all Mahajans and the inhabitants of Achleshvar, Vasishtashram, Delewada. Somsingh donated the village Dabani, (Damāni) for the maintenance of this temple but was later taken back by the Sirohi rulers. Its main sanctum, Gudhamandap and some other parts of the temple, were destroyed in 1368 V.S. (1311 A.D.) in the same year when Vimal-Vasahi was destroyed by the Musalman army. After ten years, Pethad, the son of Chandra Singh, repaired extensively this temple, at his own cost and replaced the idol of Neminath which was mutilated, by another black image of Neminath, besides three more images.

Gudhamandap

In the Gudhamandap, there are only 2 images of Jinas, now. Formerly there was placed the statue of Rajmati (Rajula), the proposed wife of Lord Neminath—standing in a centre (of the relief), with small figure of Jina, over her head, as indicated by a long inscription dated V.S. 1515 on pedestal. The statue has been removed from Gudhamandap to the cell of Ambika devi, in the corridor of this shrine. Formerly there were 26 images in the Gudhamandap, the prominent being two big sculptures of Kausaggiyas or images of Tirthankars in standing posture. These were installed by minister Dhāndhala, the follower of Nanna-acharya of Korantgaccha—a monk order. These sculptures were originally installed in Shri Mahavir Chaitya at Mundasthala Mahatirth in V.S. 1389 (1332-33 A.D.) There was also a small black image of four-armed yakhsa, with an elephant as his vehicle. They have been removed in the recent repairs.

The niches of Derani Jethani

The two famous niches, represent fine workmanship, minute chiselling and ornamentation of various types including small figures of Jinas, Jain monks, human beings, animals and birds. On the top of each is carved a sculpture of the goddess of wealth—Lakshmi Devi. In these niches are installed saparikara Panch-tirth sculpture of

Shambhavanath (the 3rd Tirthankar) and Shri Shāntinath (the 16th Tirthankar). On right hand side, in front of the above, there was in one section, a big stone Patta (slab) showing the relief images of 72 Jinas of the past, present and future ages. There is an inscription of the sixteenth century on the slab which shows that it was the gift of Shrāvika Champai (whose figure is carved out on the slab) She was Oswal by caste and native of Mandavya-gadha. This Patta has been installed in cell No 44. Col. Tod describes these two niches in the following words :

"On each side of which is a Tank or niche, partly sunk in the wall and partly projecting from it. The base is in the form of an altar over which small and very chaste columns support an exquisitely designed canopy. Though plain, nothing can surpass the execution, not an unequal line or uneven surface is perceptible. All is so finely chiselled that it appears as if moulded of wax, the edges semi-transparent, not being a quarter of a line in thickness. These niches are said to have cost a lac and a quarter of rupees or about twelve thousand pounds"

The artists were offered gold in exchange for the stone which they could eke out from the minutest work possible. Each Gokh or Gokhdā (niche) is said to have cost 9 lacs of rupees and hence they are called, Nav-Lakhi Gokhdas.

Rangamandap

In the centre of the dome, hangs a big ornamental pendant of fine carving which may be compared with the one in Vimal Vasahi.' In the words of Col. Tod. "It has more simple majesty, the fluted columns, sustaining the mandap, are loftier and the vaulted interior is fully equal to the other in richness of sculpture and superior to it, in execution which is more free and in fine taste. On the pillars supporting the mandap, are seen sixteen standing goddesses who are known as Vidyadevis. The sculpture on the pillars, torans (arches) and the domed ceiling, is simply marvellous, with finer details than those in the Rangamandap of Vimal Vasahi, although comparatively smaller in dimension. Below the Vidyadevis, on the peri-phery of the dome, are arranged in a circular band, seventy-two figures of Tirthankars in sitting postures. Below this band is another band showing 360 small figures of Jain monks. In two of the corners of the Rangamandap, are carved figures of standing deities, perhaps representing Indra. On the right side of the Rangamandap, are carved figures of twenty-four Tirthankars, on the ornamental pillars. On two of the architrave panels, between the Rangamandap and the circumbulatory passage on the western side, are carved figures of Goddess Ambikā, with attendants, on both sides.'

About the dome of the Rangamandap, Tod writes 'The dome is divided into concentric compartments by richly sculptured cordons, each intervening space being filled, with elaborate and elegant designs.' In the words of Fergusson, the eminent Archaeologist,. "It hangs from the centre more like a lustre of crystal drops than a solid mass of marble and is finished with a delicacy of detail and appropriateness of ornament which is probably unsurpassed by any similar example to be found anywhere else."

On the left of the dome, near the Pradaksina, in a ceiling is a representation of Nativity or birth of Lord Krishna. In the centre, is shown Devaki, the mother of Krishna lying on a cot, attended by two females of whom one is moving the fan. As Krishna was born in prison, therefore, the closed gates of the prison-house, are carved with beautiful figures of elephants and soldiers of Kamsa. The next ceiling near it, represents the scenes of Krishna and Gokul. Krishna was transported to the house of Nanda and Yashoda and he was brought up there. On the beam towards the east, the relief panel depicts a tree with cradle hung from its branch. Under the tree, two persons sit besides whom stands a small cowboy, with his stick held behind the neck. Above, on the self, are five vessels of milk, butter-milk and clarified butter. A bigger figure of another cow-boy standing with a stick, cattle grazing nearby and the two ladies, engaged in churning of the butter-milk, import a very realistic touch to the whole relief. By the side of the two ladies Devaki or Yashoda sits, with a child in her lap which may be either Krishna or daughter Chinnanāsha. From the swing tied to the tree, Shri Krishna tries to jump out. An elephant stands nearby whom Krishna is beating with his fists. In the same panel, Krishna is shown as uprooting two trees with both the hands. The relief on the opposite or western panel shows a king under a chattra, on a Simhasan and attended by guards and wardens. Besides stables of horses and elephants, the king's palace etc. are carved out. The stepped pyramidal roof of the two-storeyed building, to the left of the gateway, with a figure looking out of the window in each story and an open pavilion and the ground floor, one separate roof of the pavilion and one of the second story of the building, may be noted. "This figure in the half open door, is a device which the mediaeval craftsmen from Gujarat to Orissa apply by itself or else they insert it into compositions".

To the south-west of Rangamandap, in the porch, there is a ceiling representing a louts-flower, with 108 petals and each petal contains the figure of a dancing girl. This is a beautiful and unique specimen of 108 different dancing poses.

Corridor

There are 52 cells in all in the corridor, with a Hasti-

Shala, in the north-eastern corner. We would take the visitors from the left of the porch of the main entrance, facing the main sanctum and describe the important themes as we go round it. In all the cells, facing the main shrine, there are images of Jain Tirthankars, Viharmāns (Existing Jinas) of Jain mythology except in the cell of Ambamata.

In front of cell No. 1, the first ceiling shows the figure of Ambika which is mutilated but there is on each side of the goddess a tree against the stem of which stand Jain laymen and laywomen.

The second ceiling in front of cell No. 9, depicts in the centre a samavasaran with a Jina in small cell in the centre preaching sermons to Jain monks, laymen and laywomen, all standing in three different rows. On one end of this slab is shown an ocean in which are aquatic animals and boats, representing the port of Dwarkā—and the other end of the slab, shows the Jain shrines on mount Girnar with the scene of a Sangha or congregation of Jain pilgrims consisting of Sadhus (monks), Sadhvis (nuns), Shravaks (laymen) and Shravikas (laywomen), the rows of elephants, horses, devotees and dancers.

In front of cell No. 10 and 11 each of the first bays, there is a figure of goddess with a swan as her vehicle. The second bay in front of cell No. 11, shows an interesting and impressive scene of Lord Neminath in a marriage procession when he turned his chariot, at the sight of goats in an enclosure, which were meant to be killed, for his marriage feast and renunciated the world, leaving his would-be bride Rajmati who is seen sitting in a terrace with her female attendants.

The second ceiling in front of cell No. 14 contains a beautiful slab possibly relating the story of Lord Shantinath —the sixteenth Tirthankar. The slab is divided into eight sections. The first and second sections from the bottom, represent royal Hasti-Shala, Ashvashala, palace, a king with his attendants, soldiers, elephants, horses etc. The third panel depicts a figure of Lakshmi with Nava Nidhi (Nine mythical Treasures) beside her. On one side of Lakshmi, are a heap of jewels and the sun riding on saptashva (seven-headed horse) and on the other side is a beautiful elephant with moon above and a heavenly car or a palace on one side followed by an auspicious pitcher. In the rest of the panels, there are reliefs of dancers, actors, musicians, rows of elephants, soldiers etc.

In the second bay, in front of cell No. 13, there are seen two scenes from the life of Lord Pārshva Nath, the 23rd Tirthankar, the first scene represents the origin of Hasti Kalikunda Tirth (modern Ramnagar in U.P.) a sacred place where once an elephant used to worship the Lord daily with lotuses, carried in the trunk, from the kund or nearby pond after having obtained the knowledge of past life. The king Karkandu who ruled over Angadesh with Champā as the capital city. (some 2754 years ago), came to know about this wonderful devotion of an animal and went with his retinue to worship the Lord. But the Lord had left the place before the king's arrival and lamented for not obtaining Darshan or look of the Lord. While he was thus lamenting, a beautiful image of Pārshvanath came out there nine cubit in length by the supernatural power of the snake-deity Dharanendra. The king worshipped it and on this spot, erected the temple which came to be known as Hastikund Tīrth. The second scene represents Lord Parsvanath standing in meditation with a cobra, over his head, (the form assumed by the deity Dharanendra) protecting the would-be Tirthankar, from the hot rays of the tropical sun, by his snake-hoods. This place is said to be Kausamba-vana near Shivapuri. The people came in large numbers to visit it and thereafter it became famous as 'Ahichchhatranagari' and a temple dedicated to the Lord Parshvanath was also built.

Inside the cell No. 19, towards the right hand side, is placed a beautiful slab with relief representation of the story of Ashvabodh and Sakunivihar Tirth at Broach depicting important incidents from the life of Muni-suvrata Svami, the 20th Tirthankar. The slab consists of two portions—the upper one representing the story of Ashvabodha[1] (Conversion of a horse) and lower one depicting the origin of Śamali vihar Tirth.[2] A similar slab is still preserved

1. The first story runs like this that once Lord Munisuvrata Svami after attaining perfect knowledge or clairvoyant knowledge preached his sermon at Bhrghukachchha on the banks of the river Narbada and related his story as well as that of the past lives, of the horse hearing which the animal gained the supernatural cognition of its previous birth. The horse took vow not to eat or drink anything which involved killing or Himsa. This horse was let loose, by the king Jitashatru for horse-sacrifice and stayed on the way where the sermon was being preached, by Lord Munisuvrata Svami. Jitashatru, freed the horse from the bondage and it died, after observing the vow for six months and was reborn as powerful god in heaven (Śudharma-loka). He, by his super-knowledge looked to his past life and came to a place where Lord had preached his sermons. On this spot, he erected a beautiful shrine, dedicated to Shri Munisuvrata Svami and himself, in front of him as the horse-devotee.

2. The second story is like this. There was a king named Chandragupta, ruling over Ratanāshya in Simhaldvipa with capital at Shripur. His queen was Chandralekhā from whom was born a beautiful and meritorious daughter Sudarshanā. When she was grown up, a rich merchant came from the port Broach, bringing a dishful of precious stones. The merchant sneezed and to avoid ill-omen, he uttered the Jain formula,(on Namo Arihantānam). Sudarshana, soon fainted, on hearing these words. The merchant, was rebuked and given thrashing, by the courtiers in attendance at this sight. The daughter, regained her consciousness, after the treatment by the physicians. In the interval, she knew of her previous existence in which she was Samali(or Shakunika)- a kite staying on the branch of a tree, bringing some flesh to eat, after the rains of seven days and nights. She was wounded. in this state, by an arrow of a hunter and was crying in pain when all of a sudden, a Jain Muni appeared and chanted the Jain Navakar-Mantra, hearing which it breathed her last. The soul of the kite was reborn as Sudarshnā. The pious daughter, knowing her past life, became indifferent to the World, went with the merchant to Broach and worshippted

in Neminath shrine at Kumbhariyaji, some 16 miles from Abu Road and according to an inscription, it was installed in the year V.S. 1338. "A smaller but more beautiful representation of the Ashvabodha-Samlika-Vihar theme is preserved in Jain shrine at Cambay and dates from the 13th century A.D."

The replica of Ashvabodh Tirth in Lunvasahi, presents the shravakas and shravikas, the former standing with folded hands and the latter holding offerings in their hands. To the left of the attendant shravak is a smaller shrine with footprints installed in it, beyond which at the left panel is a horse standing who was imparted right knowledge, by Lord Munisuvrat Svami. To the right of the idol of Munisuvrat, is shown the king Chandragupta of Simhal-dveep with his daughter Sudarshana, seated in his lap. Adjacent to him is standing on his left, the Jain merchant Daneshwara, standing courteously with folded hands. The shrāvaka and shrāvikā, standing on the side of the shrine, may represent the king of Broach and the princess Sudarshanā coming to worship the Lord.

The lower panel shows the tree with a kite on one of its branches. The hunter shoots from one side of the tree and a figure of the dying kite, fallen on the ground is shown in front of the stump of the tree. On the other side of the tree, in front of the poor kite are two Jain monks, the front one holding his mouth-piece and the stick, in his hands while the second one carrying his stick in his right hand and the tarapani (wooden vessel) on the left. Both hold their rajoharan (broom) under the elbow. The right

there, the Ashvabodha Tirth, according to the ritual. Once upon a time, she saw the very monk who had recited her the Navakaramantra when she was a kite. She donated a large amount of wealth for charitable purposes and repaired the Ashvabodha shrine. Then, she fasted herself to death and was reborn in heaven. Therefore, the Tirth is known as Shakuni-Vihār Tirth.

half of the lower panel shows ocean in a big circle, with fishes, tortoise and such other aquatic animals and a big ship sailing ın its midst. In it is seated sudarshanā with three female attendants including one holding an umbrella over her head. The ship is also seen in a smaller size, in the winding river band which shows it entering the Broach harbour.

In cell no. 24 there is a big sculpture of the goddess Ambika, shown sitting under a mango tree with foliage spread over her head and a small Jain figure on the top of the tree. To the right side of the figure of Ambica, is placed the sculpture of Rajamati described above.

Hastishala

Beyond this, is the Hastishālā, with latticed outerwall in which is seated a magnificent saparikara sculpture of the Lord Ādināth. In front of him, is a tower of white marble stones with finely carved pillars divided into three storeys, each one containing a Jina on each of the four faces. All the sculptures of the Jinas are of black marble. On two sides of Hastishālā, are arranged in five sections, ten big elephants of superior workmanship adorned with fine tusks, trappings, the knots of the ropes, ornamental garlands, all carved out of polished white marble, each from one whole slab. These are the rare pieces of art, beautifully modelled, both realistic and stately. Below each elephant is inscribed the name of the personages who rode on its back, but the figures are all mutilated, only the traces remain. In the back wall of this Hastishālā, there are ten sections or niches in which have been installed the portrait sculptures of the Jain Acharyas udayaprabha Vijai Sen Suri, and the ancestors and descendants of Vastupal Tejpal. In the seventh and eighth niches from the left are the figures of Maham Vastupal with his two wives Shri Lalitadevi and Shri Vijaladevi and Maham Tejpal with his wife Anupamā devi. The portrait figures are shown carrying Naulis or money-purses of the old type in their hands. There are in 4 Kausaggiyas, 11 sculptures of differentt Jinas, 2 standing portraits of standing shravikas and beautiful elephants.

In cell No. 31 (30) is the sculpture of Shri Subahu, the Viharman (one of the contemporary Jinas who are twenty in number, living in the continents other than the Bharatavarsha).

In cell No. 41 (40) there was a sculpture of Lord Mahavir (now placed in cell No. 22) and adjacent to it, is a big pavilion or hall. Resting against a wall were two big loose inscribed slabs one of white and the other of black marble. They supply useful information about the family members of Vastupal and Tejpal and the trust established by them. They have been removed and preserved in Hasti-Shālā.

Girnar Tirthāvatar

Adinath, is the chief deity of Vimal-Vasahi while Nemināth is the Mulanayak of 'Luna Vasahi.' The two shrines are, therefore, known as Shatrunjaya Tīrthāvatāra and Girnar-Tīrthāvatāra respectively, because Shatrunjaya is the Tirth of Adinath and Girnār is the Tirth of Nemināth.

Luna Vasahi, being the Girnar Tirthavatar, that is, the temple of Nemināth representing the Tirth at Girnār, there are four tunks or summit cells on the top of this hill like those of Girnar. According to Arbudgiri Kalpa of Somasunder, they are known as (1) Ambāvatāra tirth (2) Pradyumnāvatāra tirth (3) Shambhāvatāra tirth and (4) Rathnemi avatāra tirth. But at present, there is only one cell containing two images of Ambika and the rest of three cells are dedicated to the worship of Parshva Nath (standing image installed in V. S. 1389), Shambhavanath (saparikar image) and unidentified Jina (black-stoned image.) These might have been replaced at the time of later repairs, sometime before 1500 V.S., in place of the images of Pradyumna, Shambhava and Rathanemi. The Girnar tunks can be approached, from the porch, outside Luna Vasahi.

After seeing the Girnar tunks, we retrace our steps and come down to the courtyard, on the left hand side. The courtyard is bedecked with the flower-beds, having a small chattri or dome of Dādā Sāhib, in which are enshrined the footsteps of the famous Kharatar gaccha Acharya Shri Jina Datt Suri, commonly known as Dādā Sāhib.

Kirti-Stambh

Turning back, after seeing the pavilion of Dādā Sāhib, we catch a glimpse of a big pillar, known as *Kīrti-Stambh,* on a raised platform, to the north-west of the courtyard. This pillar, was even bigger than what it is to-day, because, from the study of the works like Upadesh-tarangini, it appears that its top was surmounted by a representation of the hand of the mother of Shobhan Dev, the architect of Luna-Vasahi which is not existing now. This is also called by the people as 'Tirth-Stambh'. At the base of this pillar, is lying a Surahi slab, on which is engraved, the figure of a cow, with her calf and below it is an inscription of Rana Kumbha of the year V.S. 1506, which prohibits realization of any kind of tax, including escort-tax.

Col. Erskin eulogises these two temples in the followine words :—

"Amongst all this lavish display from the sculptor's chisel, two temples viz, those of Adinath and Neminath stand out as prominent and specially deserving of notice and praise, both being entirely of white marble and carved with all the delicacy and richness of ornament which the resources of Indian art at the time of their creation could devise'.

The amount of ornamental detail spread over these structures in the minutely carved decoration of ceilings, doorways, pillars, panels and niches, is simply marvellous, while the crisp thin translucent, shell-like treatment of the marble surpasses anything seen elsewhere and some of the designs are just dreams of beauty.

The general plan of the temples too, with its recesses and corridor, lends itself very happily in light and shade with every change in the sun's position."

Pittalhara or the temple of Bhimā Shah

This shrine was originally built by Bhimā Shah, of Gujarat and that is why it is called "The temple of Bhimā Shah." Nothing more than this is known about its builder. He installed a big metal image of Shri Adināth as the chief deity of the shrine which was later removed to a Jain temple at Kumbhalmer or Kumbhalgarh in Mewar. The present image weighing 108 maunds mainly of Pittala or brass was installed in V.S. 1525 (1468 A.D.) by Sundar and Gada, the ministers of Sultan Mahmud Begada of Ahmedabad. This date had led some to think that this shrine was built in V.S. 1525, but this inference does not find support in the light of the inscription of this temple of the year V.S. 1489 when this shrine was in existence. Another inscription of the year 1494 V.S., preserved in the Digamber shrine of Delwada, refers to this temple as the Pittalhar temple. So also, an inscription on the pillar of Gudhamandap of this shrine itself dated 1497 V.S. relates to the income from certain tolls, reserved for the maintenance of this shrine. Som Sunder Suri also writes in his

Arbudagiri-Kalpa in the fifteenth Century of Vikram era (1450-1499 V.S.) that Bhimā Shah, first built this temple with a metal image of Adeshvar as Mulanayak. Therefore, it may safely be concluded that this temple was in existence in V.S. 1489 (1432 A.D.). The inscriptions in the Vimal vasahi dated 1350, 1372 and 1373 show that at that time there were only two shrines—Vimal vasahi and Luna Vasahi, existing at Delwada. Thus, it may be concluded that this temple was constructed between V.S. 1373 and V.S. 1489 (1316 and 1432 A.D.)

The present image in the main sanctum was cast by an artist Deva, son of Sutradhar Madan, from Mehasana (Gujarat). The size with parikar is nearly 8 ft. in height and 5.5 ft. in breadth. The idol of Adinath itself, is 41 inches in height. The image was consecrated by Shri Lakshmi Sagar Suri. Gadā or Gadārāja, the son of the minister Sundar, spent a lac of gold coins, in consecration ceremony and in leading a Sangha on a pilgrimage to Abu.

There are about 107 images in the main shrine, Gudhamandap two niches in Nava chauki and in the corridor. In Gudhamandap, there was a sculpture of Shri Gautam Svami (the first Gandharva of Shri Mahavir) carved out of a yellow stone, with the ogha shown behind his neck, the mouthpiece on the right shoulder and a rosary (Mālā) carried in one hand. This is now placed in the right side of corridor. There is an inscription upon it on pedestal which shows that it was installed in V.S. 1509. In the corridor, there is a small temple of Lord Suvidhi Nath, the 9th Tirthankar with a pinnacle on the top. It is also mis-called as the temple Shanti nath, by the local people. To the right of saparikar image of Suvidhinath, is a beautiful figure of Shri Pundarik Svami, the chief Gandharva of Lord Adinath installed in V.S. 1394, according to the inscription on it. There is a halo around the head of Pundarik Svami sitting in Padmāsana and a lower garment is also visible.

Outside the compound of the Pitalhara temple, there is a platform round a champak tree, with a small cell of Yaksa Manibhadra.[1]

Khartar Vasahi

After passing out from the main gate of the compound of the four temples mentioned above, we see to the south-east, a three-storeyed temple of Lord Parshvanath known as Khareatar Vasahi. It seems that the latter name has been called on account of its builder being the follower of the Kharatar gaccha, an order of Jain monks. Some of the peculiarities of this order, are perceptible in this temple in the seats of the figures of Acharyas, carved here, in the popularity of images of Parshvanath.

In each story, we find Choumukh, that is, fourfold images and hence it is known as Chaumukh temple also. The inscriptions have mostly been defaced but the few letters visible, seem to suggest that most of the images were installed by sangvi Mandalik and his family of Dardā Gotra (Oswal by caste) in about 1505 V.S. From the inscriptions found in Digamber Jain temple dated 1494 V.S. and another inscription dated 1497 V.S. and another inscription dated 1497 V.S., and the surahi (memorial pillar) inscription, outside Pittalhar temple dated V.S. 1489, it is evident that Kharatara Vasahi was built after 1497 V.S. (1440 A.D.) and before 1515 V.S. (1458 A.D.) The popular belief that the masons, offered free labour, to

1. Manibhadra is originally an ancient yaksa, worshipped by Indian masses from very old times and his introduction in Jain worship as Manibhadra is only a later adaption. Yaksas, are often intimately associated with Chaitya-Vrksas (the trees of the temple) and the presence of an image of Manibhadra, near this champak tree with a platform is note-worthy.

build this temple from the remaining stones of the two temples, Vimal Vasahi and Luna Vasahi is misnomer because this shrine was not made of marble stones but of grey-stones. This three-storeyed temple, with its pinnacle, is the tallest of all temples at Delwada. A visitor from the third storey would obtain a beautiful view of the surrounding mountain ranges and the green valleys amidst them. The Mulanāyak idol is said to be Chintamani Parshvanath and on the four faces of the main sanctum on the ground floor, there are big four domes or mandaps. The outer walls of sanctum are covered with figures of Dik-Pālas (Quarter-guardians) Vidhyadevis, Yaksnis and such other deities of Jain Pantheon as Salabhanjikas. On each of the four faces, there is a big marble stone sculpture of Parshvanath, canopied by nine snake hoods and with elaborate parikara round each figure. As noticed above, the front idol is of Chintamani Parshvanath and the second of Mangalkara Parshvanath and the third of Manoratha—Kalpadruma Parshvanath, the name of the fourth figure is illegible. In front of two of these sculptures, are ornate torans or arches resting on similar pillars, while of the two others, the pillars remain but the arches above them are missing. On each of the two torans, there are representations of fifty-one figures of standing or sitting Tirthankars. Inside the temple there is dark red coloured painting of flowers etc, similar to that as in Mahavir Svami temple probably of V.S. 1821. In the corridor, there are 17 more images of Jinas.

Outside the main entrance of the sanctum on an architrave, there is a representation of Chyavana-Kalyanak Ceremony connected with descent from heaven into the mother's womb of a Jina. The mother is depicted resting on a cot and seeing the fourteen dreams which the mother of every Tirthankar, usually sees, before his birth. In front of the main temple, there is an open portico or mandap with beautifully carved dome, supported on eight simple pillars.

We reach the second storey, through a cemented staircase where there are four images, one each side. To the south, west, north and east are the images of the Tirthankars, Śumatinath, Parshvanath, Adinath, and Parshvanath respectively. All the images, were installed on Friday, the first day of the dark half of the month of Āshāda V.S. 1515. There is also a sculpture of the goddess Ambika, installed in V.S. 1515, by sangvi Māndalika, at the hands of Shri Jinachandra Suri of Kharatara gaccha. In the third storey, the images of Lord Parshvanath on each of the four sides were also installed by Sangvi Māndalika, on the same day, date and year as in the case of second storey. The inscriptions on them further show that three of them were originally installed on the second floor.

Though the stone of this temple is inferior in quality, yet the carvings of female figures, Vidhyadevis, and yaksnis, in their dancing poses with their slender waists bending down, are very superior and bold. They reflect the high workmanship of its architects. Besides, there are excellent marble columns and reliefs having rich sculpture which attract the eyes of every visitor.

On seeing all the five Jain temples, a visitor feels perfect peace of mind, experiencing detachment from the hum-drum of busy and noisy life of the plains below. The rich and beautiful sculptures, inside the two shrines namely Vimal Vasahi and Luna Vasahi, are so superb and matchless that they cannot be compared with any other place of art on marble stones. They should be considered as our national heritage and every endeavour should be made to preserve them. The approach and the surroundings of these temples with enormous hidden treasure of art and architecture, are required to be beautified and developed.

Around the Delwara Jain Temple

After visiting the famous Jain temples, we would like to take the visitors to the important places, near about them. We descend from the temple's outer platform and come down to a point, near Jain Svetamber Dharmashala, after passing through the southern gate. Then we move towards the west and going through the old hutments of Delwada, we pursue the path leading to Kanyākumāri which is situated to the north-west of the Jain temples.

Kanya-Kumari and Rasia Vālam

There are four ruined temples and one among them is known by the name of Kanya Kumari. In the shrine, there is an image of Kumwari Kanyan (Virgin lady) who is also famous as Shrīmātā (the mother goddess). There is an inscription here of the year 1497 V.S. Just opposite to it, is an open pavilion with a dome, in which is worshipped a standing male figure carrying a bowl in his left hand while on the right of the statue of Rasia Vālam, there is Trishula or tripointed spear.[1] On his right side is

1. There is an interesting and romantic legend about Rasia Valam and Kanya Kumari prevalent in the Abu region. Rasia Valam was a mystic and well-versed in magic or tantric charms.

He fell in love with the princess of a chief of Abu but the parents of the lady did not give consent to the marriage. The father put an impossible condition that if Rasia Valam was able to construct twelve different roads, on the side of Abu, to reach the top of the mountain-from its foot, within a night till the cry of the cock was heard, he would marry him his daughter. Rasia Valam, took up the challenge and started constructing and was about to complete the roads when the mother of the girl, disapproving the match, made a feigned cry of a cock, before the day-break. Hearing this Rasia Valam left his work in utter despair. Then knowing the real situation, later on, he cursed both the mother and the daughter. He threw stones over the image of the mother (which

shown a small figure of a devotee kneeling down. By the side of the statue of Rasia Valam, there is an old image of three-headed goddess, with a lion on each side as her vehicle of the sixth century A.D. (Post-Gupta age). The temple of Rasia Valam belongs to the fourteenth century.

In this area, to the South-Western side, there are a few small ruined shrines of Vishnu, Shiva and Ganesh. The Vishnu Temple is a bigger structure with a few carvings on the outerwall and some loose sculptures in its Sabhāmandap including a few figures of Hindu Mātrikās. These mātrikās and the figure of the Sūrya standing, are assignable to the post-Gupta age. A figure of Shesh Shāyi Vishnu in the shrine, is of an early age while there are two later sculptures of standing Vishnu in two niches. The repairs have been made in the fifteenth century A.D. The ruined sculptures have been kept now in the State Museum, Mount Abu.

is no more) and the heap is shown to the pilgrims. The princess turned into stone is worshipped as 'Mātā' or Kanyakumari. This version of the story is attributed to Rasia Valam who lived here and wanted to marry the virgin maid.

Besides the prevalent story, another version about the origin of Shri Mātā (Kanya Kumari) is narrated in an authoritative Sanskrit treatise 'Prabandh Chintamani. (chapter 205), written by the famous Jain Acharya Shri Manatungacharya. This work was completed by him in V. S. 1361, at Wardhvan (Kathiavar), and edited by Muni Jinavijayaji in 1940 A. D.

According to this narrative, shrīmātā was a daughter of the king Punja, the successor of the King Ratan Shekhar of Shri Ratnamal Nagar. Shrīmātā was very beautiful but her face had monkey-like appearance. Once, she recollected her past life and spoke to her father in these words "I was the wife of a monkey at Arbudgiri. My palate was pierced by a thorn while jumping from one branch of a tree to another and on account of this, my skull was separated from my trunk and the latter fell into the holy waters of Kamik Kund (pond). I was killed and born again with this beautiful body, due to the influence of the holy waters of the pond, but my skull, is still lying near this reservoir at Abu." Accordingly, the king sent his men to Abu and they submerged the skull into the pond, after its search, with the result that shrīmātā's face turned into human figure.

Nala-Gupha, Pandav-Gupha and Mauni Bava caves

From the shrine of Shrimata, walking nearly 2 furlongs to the west, there is a cave of the king Nala of Hindu mythology, and at a short distance from it, is another cave by the name of Pandav and a third one still further, is known as Mauni Bava, after the name of a monk who used to observe Mauna (silence) in this cave. These caves are not of any special interest to the visitors.

Sant Sarovar

Proceeding from Kanya Kumari, to Adhardevi, we come across, a small tank, known as *Sant Sarovar*, perhaps, after the name of a saint who might have lived there by. There is a small hermitage on its bank.

Adhardevi

As we go to the west, from Sant sarovar, we find a hilly track to reach Adhardevi. The ascent to the hill of Adhardevi is difficult one, from this side. We can climb the hill, after covering a distance of about half a mile, from

After the appearance of human face, Shrimata came to this celebrated hill and began to practise austerities. Once, an ascetic (yogi) while flying in the sky, looked down, towards this fair lady and being enticed, came upon the earth, with the intention of marrying her. Shrimata accepted his proposal on the condition that he would construct twelve staircased paths to reach Abu, before cock's cry early in the morning. The Yogi, by his supernatural power had almost completed the work of building all the twelve paths, then a feigned cry of the cock was heard. The ascetic, knowing that it was not a real cry, told her so. Thereupon, Shrimata come on the bank of a river and called him words, through her sister, for the marriage. As soon as he came enraptured with love towards her, Shrimata let loose the artificial dogs at his feet and killed him, by piercing his heart with her Trishula (a kind of spear with three—pointed heads). Afterwards, Shrimata leading a pure chaste life, died here. Her father, king Punja built a temple without sanctuary, saving it from the regular tremors of earth-quakes which were frequent, after every six months. This is the reason why the temples on this mount, have been built, mostly without any sanctuary, or big sanctuary

Delwada road, going to Mount Abu, though the ascent is not quite easy. If we start from Mount Abu and pass Nakhi lake and the Rajputana club, the ascent over the hill, starts from a well near the Kothi of the ruler of the farmer Limbdi State and we reach the temple by climbing nearly 450 steps.

The image of the Goddess Adhardevi, or Arbudā Devi, is enshrined in a small cave. She is said to be the superintending goddess of the whole of Mount Abu. The entrance to the cave is very low and the visitor has to bend down to gain entrance to the shrine. Just close to the cave, is small temple of Shiva with a small cave and a rest house or Dharmashala. The fair is held twice a year, on the full moon day of Chaitra and Ashvin month. The temple is called as Adhardevi, because the image of the deity, is hanging without any support on either side and a cloth could pass underneath but now a thread can pass only. It is believed that there are some magnetic properties in the stone which keeps it, without any support.

Papakateshvara Mahadev

From Adhardevi, if we ascend half a mile higher, we come to Papakateshvara Mahadev, in dense forest. There is Shiva linga, with a small kund (pond) under a mango tree and a cave nearby. It is believed by the Hindus that at the sight of Shiva linga all past sins are destroyed.

Trevor Tank

From Delwada Bus Stand, just situated adjacent to the state Dak-Bungalow, after walking a short, distance on Delwara Achalgarh road and passing by '*Lāl Math*' with red-coloured shrine, we move to the left and take a circuitous bye-road which leads to Trevor Tank. The distance from the turning point is about a mile. There are dense forests on both sides of the road on which the private cars and taxis can ply well. Trevor Tāl or Trevor Tank is a fine lake named after Col. Trevor who was formerly Agent to the Governor-General, Rajputana. It was built in 1894-95 A.D., at the cost of nearly Rs. 35,000 with the object of supplying drinking water to Abu, but this scheme failed. The Abu Municipality has laid down the side parks and repaired the rest house, situated on its bank. The lake is surrounded by wooded slopes and luxuriant trees which convert this artificial lake into a beautiful spot of nature. This is a good place for picnic.

Guru-Shikar

Returning from the same route, we join the Delwada-Achalgarh road and covering a distance of about 3 miles, we come to the Oria Hotel from which a path goes to Guru-Shikar, which is the highest peak of Abu. It is 5650 feet above the sea-level. We go to Guru-Shikar, by the hamlet Javāi and the path is difficult through a range of hills and rocks. On this way, there are Shiva temple, Kama Kund and Gau-Shala with a small garden. Proceeding further onwards, we reach the small temple of Guru Dattātreya on the high peak of the rock. Every year, pilgrims flock to this place, regarding Dattātreya, as an incarnation of God Vishnu. There was an old bell with an inscription of 1468 V.S. which was broken and was replaced by a new bell. It is said that the old bell is preserved by the Mahant of the shrine. A little to the north-west of it, is another peak with a shrine of Ahalyā, the mother of Guru Dattātreya. Nearby there is a Dharmashala with a small cave wherein lives the Mahants and other Sadhus. From the peak, the visitors can cherish fine view of Abu. The glimpse of Sirohi and Ambika Devi shrine on another hill of Aravalli range can be had, from the high peak. The visitors can descend a little on the other side, with a guide to a place known as *Ganesh-Nālā*, a beautiful lovely, spot, with dense growth of trees in valleys around it. From here a road leads to Uttraja, an ancient village. From this way we can come back to Guru Shikar by Ganesh nala. The path is, no doubt, difficult but the wild natural scenery is fine and enchanting.

Oria

We return from Gurushikar to the Oria Hotel and then walking a short distance, we come to Dak-bungalow, near village, Oria. The distance from Oria Hotel to Oria is about half a mile. In Oria, there is an old and big Jain temple of Shri Mahavir Svami, built probably in the 15th century. Today, the chief deity of the temple is Adinath. Shri Somsunder Suri, in his Arbudgiri-Kalpa composed towards the close of the fifteenth century V.S., mentions that there was the worship of Shri Shantinath in the newly built Jain shrine at Oriyāskapur (Oria). It seems that originally the shrine was built towards the first half of fifteenth century V.S. (1400—1450 A.D.) and that originally an image of Shantinath was installed as Mulanayak and in later repairs, a new image of Shri Mahavir might have been installed as the chief deity whereupon people called it a shrine of Mahavir. The Hindu temples of Koteshevar (Kanakhaleshvar) and Chakreshvar Mahadev are situated at the southern outskirts of the village. There is an inscription of 1265 V.S., when the renovation ceremony of this temple took place. It lies in ruins now. The sanctum and two chowkis in front, are in existence while the compound of the shrine etc. is totally destroyed. In the temple, there is shiva linga and the image of Parvati, and in the niches of the ancient hall are the figures of Ganesh and other gods. This is considered to be a holy

Tirth of Hindus. It was repaired, as said above, on Vaishahka Shukla 15 V.S. 1265, by a Shaiva monk Kedar, Rishi, a pupil of Durvāsā Rishi, when Dhara Varsha, feudatory chief of the Solanki king Bhimdev II was governing this area. Nearby are Bhima-Gupha (a big hollow in the rock) under the shade of a banayan tree. If we descend a few steps we find a reservoir, by the name of sakkara (sugar) kunda. Its water is very sweet to taste.

Achalgarh

About a mile and a half, from Oria and 4 miles from Delwada, there is village of Achalgarh, situated on a small hill, with fortification, built by Rana Kumbha. On the ascent, there are Ganesh Pol (the image of Ganesh being on the right hand side), Hanuman Pol, (having a cell dedicated to Hanuman, on the left). Then, starts the ascent upwards, built with stones and concrete. On our left, is the small tank of Kapursagar, full of cool waters, during all the seasons of a year and small garden adjacent to it, managed by Svetamber Jain Managing committee. Then, further we come to Champa Pol, with a small Shiva shrine, after passing by the small temple of Laxmi Narain. Going through this entrance, we reach the old Jain Karyalaya in which is situated the temple of Shri Kunthunath, the seventeenth Tirthankar. A little upwards, is Bhairon Pol with a small image of Bhairava at its entrance. Still upwards is the present office of Seth Achalsi Amarsi Pedhi (HQ S. Roheda), together with Dharmashala and Bhojanashala providing facilities of boarding and lodging to the Jain pilgrims.

By the side of the office, a road goes upwards to the Achalgarh Fort, passing by an Ashrama and a cell of Vijai Shanti Suri, a well-known Jain monk who used to meditate here. Near the doorway of this Ashram, on the left wall, there is an idol of Bhairava, from which the gateway now fallen, took its name (the sixth gateway in ascent). Going still upwards, we come to two kunds or tanks known as Shrāvana and Bhādara, on the names of the Hindu calendar months. These tanks remain filled up with water throughout the year and near by is the shrine of the goddess Chamundā. On the top of the hill, there is an old fort of Rana Kumbha in ruins. Descending from it, at a short distance, one finds two-storeyed cave, associated with the Puranic king Harish Chandra or at times of Gopichand—a monk of Nāth School. A little further, another downward path from the cave, goes to an old palace of Rána Kumbha.

The Achalgarh fort was built by Rana Kumbha of Chittorgarh (Mewar) in V.S. 1509 (1452-53 A.D.) and the Rana often used to live here. It remained in his pessession for sometimes after 1441 A.D. seizing it from the Deoras of Sirohi. Col. Tod has described the fort in these words. "The upper fortress, is attributed to Kumbha. But he, probably, only repaired this, the denizen of Achal garh, which, with the interior work, is of the most remote antiquity. There are the ruins of a grainary, the Bhandar of Kumbha Rana, coated within, with a very strong cement. Close on the left is the palace of Oka Rani, his queen, so designated from being of oka Mandal, near the Land's End of the Hindus. On the most elevated knell to the east are the remains of an alarm tower which still bears Kumbha's name". This fort was once inhabited by rich and pious Jains and also by Rajputs, Brahmins, merchants and artisans and was in flourishing state. But now, it is crumbling down and except for Achalgarh Jain shrines, there is probably no habitation. The higher peaks of Achalgarh command a magnificent view of the distant surrounding plains, with river Banās and the green fields on its banks. This fort, also remained the capital, of Parmars and Chauhan rulers of Chandravati and Sirohi during the war time being the safest place, among the rocks and hillocks of mountain.

Achalgarh Jain Shrines

Passing through the entrance of Jain Pedhi Office, we go upwards to the famous Chaumukh shrine of Shri Adeshvar Bhagvan, built by Singvi Sahasā, of Prāgvāt (Porvad) community. He installed a very heavy big metal sculpture weighing nearly 120 mounds to the north as the principal deity in V.S. 1566, at the hands of Shri Jaya Kalyan uri, with a big festival celebrated by Sangvi Asā, the cousin brother of Singvi Sahasā. The latter, spent lacs of rupees, in building the shrines at such a height and in leading a Sangha of pilgrims to Achalgarh. The inscription of this description is engraved on the pedestal of the image.

Being Chaumukh shrine, there are four idols on four directions. The image to the east, is a big metal sculpture of Shri Adeshvar and was installed on the 4th day of Vaishakha dark half of the year 1518 V.S., by Shah Shalhā (Oswal), the Chief Minister of Somadas, the ruler of Dungarpur and its consecration ceremony was performed by Shri Laxmi Sagar Suri of Tapogaccha. The image was cast by the artists, Lumbha, Lampa and others of Dungarpur. On the southern side, there is an idol of Shri Shantinath the big bronze image, gifted by Shravika Karmade, the mother of the minister Shah Salha, for the spiritual benefit of her husband Shah Sābhā and installed in the year V.S. 1518 at Dungarpur. On the western side, there is the image of Shri Adeshvar Bhagvān, installed in V.S. 1526 by Shah Salha. The last two images were brought here from Komulmer or Kumbhalgarh in Mewar.

All the four images have some art and design and are akin to each other.

On two sides of the Mulanayak are seen the two big beautiful bronze scriptures of Tirthankars, having inscriptions of the year V.S. 1134 (1078-79 A.D.). In the main sanctum, there are besides 4 principal bronze images, two big bronzes of standing Jinas, one stone image of a sitting Jina and two big stone sculptures of standing Jinas, bearing different dates on their pedestals.

On the walls of the sabhamandap, there are beautifully painted Pattas of Jain holy places. To the right and left hand sides, are the small cells of the Lord Parshva nath (installed in V.S. 1698) and Lord Neminath (installed in V.S. 1518). In the Bhramati or circumbulatory passage, passing by a Chattri pavilion of stone Patta (slab) of nine footprints of different Jain monks, we ascend to the upper floor (second storey) where there are another Chaumukh images (cast from brass or bronze metal) of Parshvanath and Adinath, having inscriptions dated V.S-1566 A.D. In this shrine, there are fourteen bronze images (12 of sitting Jinas and 2 of standing) which weigh nearly 1444 maunds, according to the popular belief.

On a lower level than the above Chaumukh shrine, there is another temple dedicated to Adinath, installed in the year 1721 V.S. (1665 A.D.) and it was gifted by Doshi Shantidas of Ahmedabad. Shrimali by caste, the temple itself was erected by Shantidas some 200-300 years before. In the Bhramati of this temple, there are 24 smaller cells, 4 chattris with footprints etc., one cell dedicated to the goddess Ambika. Out of these, four Chattris and the cell of Ambika are older and the idol of Sarasvati, the stone Chakra, a very beautiful image of a Yaksa (probably Manibhadra) are worthy of mention. It appears that the worship of Sarasvati existed in Achalgarh from olden times.

The shrine of Kunthunath

As said above, this temple is situated, in the compound of the old office of Jain svetamber Karkhana. It looks like Grha-Derāsar or a temple in a private residence. There is in the temple, a beautiful bronze image of Shri Kunthunath, the seventeenth Tirthankar installed in the year V.S. 1527 (1470 A.D.). There are 173 Jina images including mostly the metal images of smaller sizes, called Dhātu Pratimas. In the second storey, above the old Karkhana Office, there is a room where a portrait (penpicture) of late Acharya, Shri Shanti Surija, has been placed, marking the place where the Yogi-Raj the renowned figure breathed his last. He commanded a large following of Jains and people of other sects. Many of the ruling princes, bowed him as their Guru. He passed away in the winter of 1942 A.D. In the old office of the Jain Pedhi, are placed three beautiful equestrian bronze figures of three horsemen, each figure weighing 2 maunds and costing 100/- Mahmud (silver) coins. The rider with the umbrella, on his back, represents Dharma Raja Dattaraja, son of Kalki Avatar (incarnation according to the Hindu legends) and other riders represent some Kshtriya Chief of the former Sirohi state. The former figure was the gift of Shah Shārdūla and his father, Shah Panna of Kumbhalgarh fort in Mewar, during the reign of Rana Kumbha in V.S. 1566 and the other two were presented in the same year, for being placed in the same shrine built by themselves.

The Shrine of Shanti Nath

There is an ancient temple which is to be seen on descending the Achalgarh fort. It lies to the left side on the road leading to Delwara. The shrine itself is said to have been built by Solanki Raja, Kumar Pal of Gujarat.

The references are found in Arbuda Kalpa (in the Vividha Tirth Kalpa of Jina Prabhsuri) and Arbudgiri Kalpa of Som Sunder Suri, about a shrine on Mt. Abu, dedicated to Shri Mahavir Svami, by the King Kumar Pal of Gujarat. This temple and its references lead us to believe that this was the temple built by Kumar Pal, because there was no other temple, existing on Abu, by the name of Kumar Pal. It is just possible that there was the idol of Mahavir Svami and it might have been broken and mutilated during Muslim invasions and the present idol of Shantinath might have been placed instead.

The shrine faces the East and it consists of the sanctum the Gudhamandap (hall), Nava chowki, the Sringar-Chowki and a court-yard, all in one compound, encircled by strong walls. The sculpture of the sanctury, is very artistic and attractive. On the basement of this shrine, are obtained the mouldings with rows of quadrupeds, elephants, lions, human beings etc. It seems to have been built by the same king, probably by Kumar Pal. "The narathara of the basement moulding is especially interesting with different motifs carved in small figures, including those of standing and sitting Tirthankaras, Acharyas and monks; wrestling scenes, march of armies, figures of the five Pandavas, processions and so on. All the sidewalls of the sanctum and the adjoining front hall, have fine carvings of Jinas and big relief of gods and goddesses."

In the garbhagraha in front of Mulanayak, is finely wrought toran (arch) with two pilasters on which are carved out some miniature figures of Tirthankars.

The chief image of the shrine, is a big sculpture with attendant parikara, well-carved and beautiful in appearance. In the Rangmandap, there are two big stone sculptures of standing Tirthankaras, having on each of them, 23 more miniature Jina figures carved on the three sides of the standing Jina, each sculpture is thus a Chovisi sculpture. One of them has an inscription dated V.S. 1302, This finishes the description of the Jain temples at Achalgarh.

The temple of Achleshvar Mahadev

From the temple cf Shantinath, we come to the ancient temple of Achleshvar Mahādev an ancient Hindu shrine of Shiva, the Hindu God. It is said to have been built in 813 A.D. In this temple, the sanctity is attached to the toe of God Shiva which has attracted countless devotees ever since. Below the emblem, there is a hole of immeasurable depth which goes right to Pātāl (the innermost core of the earth). The famous king Dhārāvarsh doubted its truth and he poured water, to test its efficacy, but in vain. The God's curse fell on him and he was the last ruling Parmar Chief.

Achleshwar Mahadev, is supposed to be the superintending deity of Mount Abu. The God was worshipped as the tutelary deity, by the Parmar chief of Abu and the Chouhan rulers of Sirohi. According to the Hindu traditions, the temple is very ancient and it underwent numerous repairs from time to time, as pointed out by many inscriptions in the shrine. The temple consists of Mulagarabhagraha, (main sanctum) Sabhamandap and a very wide courtyard. In the main sanctum, besides the toe of Shiva, there is the niche on the back wall on which is enshrined the sculpture of goddess Parvati, the wife of Lord Mahadev. In the sabhamandap, on the right corner, there is a marble slab of 108 Shiva lingas of small size. It also contains a number of small images of different gods and goddessess, out of these, a small figure of Mahishamarddini is assignable to the 8th century A.D. The inscriptions in the hall, belong to the period from the 13th to 18th century A.D. In the compound, there are the temples of

Lakshminarayan, cell of Chamunda devi, 16 other cells of different sizes and 7 ruined platforms with Shiva lingas, images of Ganesh, Parvati and others.

In the Lakshminarayan temple, there are figures of ten incarnations of Vishnu, including the figure of Buddha as one of them and sculptures of Vishnu resting on the serpent Shesha (Shesh Shayi Vishnu). There is a big inscription on the right wall of the shrine relating to Vastupal and Tejpal dated V.S. 1294 which suggests that the Sabhamandap of Achleshvar shrine was constructed by these two brother ministers, in V.S. 1290 (1234 A.D.) This is supported by Vastu Pal Charitam of Jina Harsha Gani (Sarga 8 V. 17) and Vastupal Tejpal Prabandha (Puratan Prabandha Samghra (Singhi series P. 53), Though devoted Jains, they had liberal outlook towards other sects. In 1348 V.S. (1292 A.D.), Maharawal Samar Singh of Mewar, also repaired the monastery of the temple, at the instance of its saint, Bhava Shankar. He also raised a golden staff, on the shrine and made donations and arrangements for free meals for hermits residing in this monastery. An inscription dated V.S. 1377, lying in a niche outside the shrine, refers to the Conquest of Abu and Chandravati by Chauhan Chief Maharav Lumba and gives geneology of Chauhan princes. The inscription of Maharav Tej Singh, of V.S. 1387, suggests that the step-well behind Achleshvar temple, was constructed by him. Just near the main shrine there is a Toran (arch) from which scales used to be suspended to weigh the rulers of Sirohi, against gold, silver, corn etc. and these articles were given to the poor and needy. This was called Tulā-dān or charity by weighing oneself in the scales.

Just, in front of the shrine, there is preserved a big brass figure of bull-vehicle (Nandia) of Shiva, installed in V.S. 1464 according to the inscription on the pedestal. It bears the mark of violence on its flanks. The tale runs that Md. Begra injured it in search of treasure but while he was leaving, Shiva let loose swarm of bees on his retreating force and they had to run away. The valley down which he fled, is still called *Bhamar Bhāttā.* Outside the cell, is a very big trident of iron which is the gift of Rana Lakha, Thakur Madan and Kunwar Bhādā. It was fashioned in the village of Ghanerav and offered to the shrine. An Annual fair, is held once a year, on the last day of the dark half of Chaitra when people of all sects gather for the worship of God Shiva.

Mandakini Kund

Near the Achleshvar Temple, there is a big tank measuring 900 ft. long and 240 feet broad, by the name of Mandakini Kund, the water of which is supposed to be sacred as that of the Ganges. Such extensive kunds are rare. We find many kunds and ponds, of exquisite designs at Chittorgarh also which remained the ancient capital of Mewar, but they are not so extensive as it is. This kund is now lying in ruins. It is not definitely known when it was originally built. In this connection, Mahamahopadhyaya Gauri Shankar Ojha, the famous historian of Rajasthan, refers to the Prashasti of the Chittor-Kirti-Stambh which says that Maharana Kumbha, built here the temple of Kumbha Svami and a kund nearby. This temple of the Rana, now in ruins, is situated on the northern end of the kund and therefore it is probable that Rana Kumbha might have repaired it. A legend is prevalent that this kund was full of ghee, in the old days. Three demons, in the form of three buffaloes used to steal ghee from the tank at night. The Parmar Chief Dharavarsha killed these three buffaloes with his arrow and pierced all the three, by one aim. The statues of the buffaloes (with holes) and Dharavarsha, are still to be seen, standing on the side of the kund.

The Statue of Dharavarsha

The statue of Dharavarsha, the Parmar ruler of Abu, is very beautiful. He is seen standing and making an aim with his arrow, charged on a stretched bow. It is said that Dharavarsha was so brave and skilled in the art of archery that he could pierce three buffaloes, standing in one line. There was an inscription, on the plinth of the pedestal of this statue, the most material part of which has been effaced.[1] There was fragmentary inscription on the bow dated V.S. 1533, which is not existing today.

I could only read the year V.S. 1533 and the month Phālgun and the date the 6th dark fortnight and the day Wednesday; as well as the words 'Ālha's Son'; and 'Devada Parmar', on the pedestal of the statue.[2] It seems that the figure is older and the inscribed part of the bow might have been mutilated and replaced by another on pedestal, in V.S. 1933. The portrait sculpture, is 5 ft. high and is similar to the sculptures of Vastupal and others in Luna Vasahi.

Sarneshvar Mahadev

On the western bank of the kunds, is the temple of Sarneshvar Mahadev, built in the memory of Maharav Man Singh of Sirohi, who was treacherously killed on Abu, by some Parmar Rajputs and was cremated on the site of this temple. His mother, Dhārābai, built this temple in the year 1634 V.S. In it are enshrined, the Shiva linga,

1. Col. Tod : Travels in Western India pp. 90

2. आल्हा सुत संवत् 1533 फाल्गुन मासे कृष्ण पक्षे 6 बुध वासरे देवड़ा परमार वर लंघ प्रतिष्ठा करापितं संघ।"

and image of Parvati in the niche behind the linga and in the wall, a sculpture representing Man Singh with his five queens.

The Cave of Bhartrihari

At a little distance, from the northern bank of Mandakini Kund, is a cave known as the *cave of Bhartrihari*, after the renowned king Bhatrihari. It is now included in a recently erected building which is believed to be built by Bhima Shah who built Pittalhar shrine at Delwada.

Revati Kund

To the east of Mandakini Kund, there is another small reservoir known as Revati Kund, at a distance of about a quarter of a mile. It always, remains full of sweet and cool water. It appears to be an ancient kund with flight of steps on two sides and the remaining two sides formed of natural rocks.

Bhrgu Ashram

About half a mile from Revati Kund to the east, is *Bhrgu Ashram* where there is a Shiva linga and an image of Parvati, and a small step-well and a kunda, in which the water percolates from a natural outlet through an artificial Gaumukh or cow-mouthed water pipe. In front of the Shiva temple under the shade of a Champak tree, there is a small platform with a pavilion or Chattri in which is seated a small image of the four-faced Hindu Brahma and a pair of footprints. There is also a figure of Ganesh in the niche of the step-well.

Shri Tirtha Vijaya Ashram

On a slightly higher level than the Bhrgu Ashrama, and at a short distance from it, there is a small quarter, consisting of a hall and a verandah in front, with an open terrace above. It was used by Yogiraja Shri Shanti Suri at whose behest it was built in memory of Shri Vijai Kesara Suri. From this place, an excellent view of Chaumukh shrine is obtained. This Ashram itself is also surrounded by natural sights.

MOUNT ABU

Dudhavavadi

After visiting Achalgarh, we descend and come to Mount Abu, passing through Oria Hotel and Delwara Bus-stand. On the way, near the foot of the flight of steps leading to Adhardevi, there is a well by the name of '*Dudnavavadi*'. The water of this well is whitish and sweet like milk. There are also two or three quarters for the Hindu monks to stay in.

Nakhi Lake

From Dudhavavadi, there is straight road of about a mile to Nakhi Lake, passing by Limbdi House and Brahma Kumaris Ishvariya Visva Vidyalaya, Pandava Bhavan. We would, better, take the visitors, from the turning point of Delwara Abu Road, near vakilvilla, and passing by Rajputana club, Power House, Central Police Training College, Post Office and then to Nakhi Lake, after moving to the right. From the Power house, a road also goes to the Post Office via Raj Bhavan (the Governor's House). Nakhi Lake is about a mile from the straight road and about a mile and a half from the common road.

According to the Hindu legend, long long ago there was a Bashkali—a wicked demon. He became so arrogant, overbearing and tyrannous that all the sacrifices in the world ceased. In their distress, the gods called on Brahmā—the creator of universe—who counselled that they should all go to the holy hill of Abu and there undergo great austerities. The gods performed what they were called for. They dug out a deep pit with the nails of their hands to dwell in, for protection against the diabolical devices of the wicked demon. This pit, is called "Nakhi Lake" being dug out from the finger nails of gods. Today, it is considered as a place of sanctity, by the Hindus. They perform pilgrimage, by going round it, by drinking its water and bathing in it. The Municipal Board, Abu has prohibited fishing, washing and cleaning on the ghats near the camp Bazar or the temples on its banks. It is now, more a beauty spot than a mere sacred place, for the visitors. Col. Tod described it, about 400 yards in length while Fergusson, an eminent authority on Indian Architecture, said that it was exquisitively beautiful. It is surrounded by hills at a respectable distance. The lake is about half a mile long and a quarter of a mile broad and 20 to 30 feet deep towards the dam on the west. Several rocky islands, fringed with superb palm trees, have added beauty to this charming lake while the grand and handsome palaces of the former ruling princes, beautiful Hindu temples and crowded bathing ghats in its vicinity, enhance its beauty too. Mahatma Gandhi's ashes were brought here and immersed in this holy lake, on 12th February 1948. The Gandhi Ghat, has been newly constructed, with green lawns and colourful flower-beds on its bank. The steam boats and other kinds of boats, ply in the lake, being arranged by the Municipal Board Abu, for the visitors, on cheap rates. To the east of the lake is the palace of the former ruler of Jodhpur state and to the south-west, the Jaipur Palace, a beautiful and splendid building on the mount. Then, there are the temples of Shri Raghunathji and Duleshvar Mahadev, on its banks. It is said that there once existed a Jain Temple also, on the side of the lake.

The Temple of Raghunathji

On the South-Western bank of Nakhi Lake, there is the temple of Raghunathji where there is provision for lodging and boarding specially for the Hindus. It is the chief centre of the followers of the sect of Ramanand, a great monk who lived in the fourteenth century A.D. Svami Ramanand (living between 1300 to 1449 A.D.) built the original temple and installed the idol of Shri Raghunathji (Lord Rama), which he got from one sage named Bhalindasunu who used to practise austerities on the mount. It was renovated recently by its mahants, the present mahant being Svami Ram sobhagdasji Vaishnava Guru. The temple has a big and extensive compound. The main shrine itself is of white marble stone with the images of various Hindu gods, in the Sabha Mandap or hall outside the principal sanctum. A fine dome has been erected over Sabhamandap. The idol of Raghunathji is black, beautiful and very nicely decorated. Every year, on the fifth day of the bright half of the month of Phalgun, the annual function of the renovated temple is held and on these festival days, the visitors are exempted from payment of pilgrim tax, by the Municipal Board, Abu. The temple occupies a commanding site and a fine and attractive view of the lake is obtained from it.

Duleshvar Temple

Between the Raghunathji temple and the palace of the Jaipur ruler, there is a Shiva temple famous as Duleshvar Mahadev, besides which there is Ashram (rest house) for monks.

Champa Gupha

At some height, from Raghunathji Temple, on a hill there are two or more caves under the shade of Champak trees growing nearby. They are, therefore famous as 'Champa Gupha'. Nakhi Lake presents a lovely sight from this place.

Rama Jharokha

Still further from Champa Gupha, is a spot where there are two caves looking like Gavāksh or Jharokhā and hence both are known as Ram-Jharokha.

Toad Rock

On hill to the south-west of the Raghunathji temple, there is a rock which looks like a frog hence it has been named as the Toad rock.

Hasti-Gupha

At a little distance from Rama Jharokha, is a delightful spot of Hasti-Gupha. The broad upper part of the cave looks like an elephant and therefore, it has been named as Hasti-Gupha.

Ram-Kund

From Hasti-Gupha, at a short distance is Ram-Kund a small well, the water of which never dries up. There is a shrine of Lord Ram Chandra with the images of Rama, Lakshman and Sita installed in it.

Gorakshini Mata

At some distance from Hasti-Gupha, is the site of Gorakshini Mata (the goddess who protects cattle). A fair is held in Phalgun (spring season) annually there.

The Sun-Set Point

Retracing our steps backwards and coming to the tri-junction of roads, by Raghunathji Temple and Dulesh-war Temple, we move by South-west road to the sun-set point, keeping the Pologround to the left. The distance is about a mile from the Pologround. The private taxis and cars can ply over this road. To obtain the distant view of the setting sun, downwards in the plains, the visitors climb the hillocks and take their seats, on raised platforms, stone-chairs specially built for the purpose. The visitors, after taking their seats, wait anxiously to see the sun, appear-ing to be sinking beyond the horizon. Nearer the sun to-wards, the horizon, the greater the charm and interest of the natural phenomena, which occur every clear and cloudless evening. Before the sun sets in with fading lustre, it fills the sky with various colours, of the rainbow and "the Abu hills with their natural surroundings and the plains below are filled with certain spiritual calm which a visitor silently watching the sun-set, does not like to disturb. The age-old Mount Abu, like an old Indian Yogi sitting in deep meditation, undisturbed from the rise and fall of nations and cultures of empires and individuals from several millenium past, by its sheer silence, laughs at our little vanities of life, piercing even the most gaily attired blonde (returning from the sunset point) with a sheer cold breeze, and leaving a deep-set gloom, stamped on her face."

Trevor Oval or Pologround

From the sunset point, we return to Trevor Oval or Pologround, which is a vast playground. It was formerly the Pologround. It, is now, regularly used by The Central Police Training College. The passing out parade of I.P.S. officers and other sports are staged here. The annual functions are also held here. It has a pavilion also, called as 'Polo Pavilion'. The Municipal office and Municipal Cinema are situated at stone's throw from pologround.

Bus-Stand and Shānti Sadan

In front of Trevor Oval or Pologround, towards the eastern side, there is the S.T.C. Bus Stand, Mount Abu and the office of the Railway out-agency and in the upper storey, there is Tourist Bureau. Further, to the right side of the road going to Abu Road, there is a double-storeyed building, with fine quarters equipped with necessary facilities like beds, utensils etc. for catering the needs of the visitors. This is known as Shānti-Sadan.

Abu Sanatorium or Abu Camp Area

If we move towards the north, from Bus Stand, we come across, the main Bazar, Post and Telegraph Office, Rajasthan State Offices, Vishram Bhavan Sanatorium Hindu Hotels, lodges, Raj Bhavan in which is situated State Museum, open for the public, the offices of The Survey of India, Western Circle, The Central Police Training College, Rajputana Hotel, Rajputana Club, Nun-Rock, Lawrence School and Churches, Idgah, Abu High School, St. Mary's Boys' High School, Nilkanth Mahadev, and Military Barracks. It is needless to mention the names of the afore-mentioned institutions as they themselves indicate the purpose for which they are meant, except the Nun-rock, situated, by the side of the Tennis courts of the Rajputana Club and Nilkanth Mahadev. The rock is called Nun-rock as it appears like a Christian nun praying with folded hands. One more ancient place worth mentioning, is Nilkanth Mahadev, on the Mount Abu-Delwara Bus-route. The temple is very ordinary one, but the Shiva linga has abnormal dimension and it is said that such a lingum has not been found, after the 10th century.

The Descent

After visiting the important places on Mount Abu, we would descend the hill and mention the important places, situated on the roadside and even at some distance from it. The legend describes that Rasia Valam, built 12 roads to this hill, during one night as mentioned before, through the influence of his magic. But, we have nothing to say about it, as it may be a myth only. At present there are three routes besides some slopes which descend down from the Abu hill to the plains below. The first route turns from Idgah and goes down to Gaumukh, Vasishtashram and Jamadagni Ashram and other places. The second one goes from Anādra Gate to Anādra and the third is the common Bus route from Mount Abu Bus Stand to Abu Road.

We would take the first route which is hilly and hazardous but enjoyable as it passes through wild dense forests. It is not the common route to reach the plains and the visitors would avoid it, after seeing the ancient Ashrams of the Rishis. From Idgah near mile No. 1 on the main bus-road, from Mount Abu, we walk down a distance of about 1½ miles and reach Hanuman Ashram, passing by St. Xavier College, a newly constructed building on a hill.

Hanuman Ashram

The place Hanuman Ashram is so called because of the idol of Hanumanji—the monkey God which is worshipped here. A small fruit-garden, is maintained by a mahant living here. The Abu municipality, has also built a shed here, for the comfort of the visitors to and from Gaumukh and has also extended the water pipe line to this Ashram. This is the half way house, for the visitors and pilgrims going to Gaumukh and Vasishta-Ashram.

Gaumukh

A little further from Hanuman Ashram, we descend about 700 old and worn out stone steps, amidst shady trees and plants of wild fragrant flowers and come to Gaumukh. It is a rectangular reservoir, with symmetrical steps on its four sides, in which the water of everlasting spring flows through the mouth of the marble cow, facing the west and fixed in the eastern wall of the pond. The water of this place is considered sacred and the Hindus take dip into it. This lovely spot, is surrounded by sweet scented Ketaki and Mogra flower plants. In the summer, the sweet and lusty fragrance, coming out of the mango trees, delights the visitors. To the left of the marble cow-mouth, is the image of God Ganesh and to the right of it is an inscription of V.S. 1707 which is not readable being white-washed. There, is still another inscription of V.S. 1875 (the month Magh) from which it appears that the embankment or Pāl existed from the times of Parmars and the Vasishta temple and Gomati kund, from the times of Vasishta and Badrinath shrine on Gaumukh kund, was built by Maharav Shiva Singh of Sirohi and the heir-apparent Guman Singh, at the cost of Rs. 10.000 and its consecration ceremony was held on Vaishkha Shukla 15, V.S. 1874. Above the kund, there are two small cells or chattris. In one of them, we find the liṅga of Koteshvar Mahadev and the beautiful idol of Vishnu (chaturbhujaji) 4 ft. × 1½ ft. Besides, there are two small images of other gods. Perhaps, this shrine of Vishnu, might be the Badrinath shrine referred to above. In the other cell, is placed a beautifully carved out sculpture of Shesh Shayi Vishnu of the size of about 1½ ft. × 1 ft.

Vasishta Ashram

Still downwards, at a very short distance, is the famous

place known as Vasishtā-Ashram with the main shrine of Vasishta, the family priest of Lord Rama and his brother Lakshman—the heroes of Ramayana. It is said that the sage Vasishta, used to live here in this Ashram or hermitage long ago—The temple was built during the times of Maharav Kanhad Dev, the son of Maharav Tej Sinha who was the son of the Chauhan ruler Lumbaji of Chandravati. In the shrine, is also seen an image of the Arundhati, the wife of Rishi Vasishta along with the two brothers, Rama and Lakshman. Also, in the temple are the idols of Garuda, the god of flying birds and the god Hanuman. The entrance is towards the south and the two pillars of the doorway, are very finely carved out. Outside the doorway and facing the temple, in the right wall are set three inscriptions and on the left, only one. The right wall inscriptions are of V.S. 1394, 1506 and 1589. The first one, dating from V.S. 1394 (Vaisakh Sudi 10, Thursday) describes the times of Maharav Kanhada Dev who granted the village Veervādā for the maintenance of this temple while his father Tej Sinha, gifted the villages of Zabatum (zanbatum), Jyatuli and Tejalpur. The second, just below it, of V.S. 1506 (Ashadh Sudi 11, Thursday), mentions that Rana Kumbhakaran (Kumbha), son of Mokul, donated the village Khursadi or Kharādi (the modern Abu Road), for maintenance of the temple. The third inscription dated V.S. 1589 (Vaisakh Sudi 15 Thursday) relates that during—the times of Maharaj Shri Ashiraj, Gaumukh and its Pāl (embankment) were constructed by Raimal. The Gaumukh inscription refers the construction of the embankment to the Parmar king and therefore it may be believed that the Pāl was built by Parmar King Raimal.

The inscription on the left wall of V.S. 1514 (Vaisakh Sudi 9, Saturday) mentions about Vasishta, his wife

Arundhati and the name of the architect Lakhmā. Further, on this slab which is not clearly readable, there is inscribed the year V.S. 1523, month Chaitra Sudi 15, Friday against the name of Maharana Khetā and Bhandari Heera. The exact significance of it could not be made out.

In the front of the temple, are the small cells of Indra, the god of rains, Lakshmi Narain, and some foot-prints. Towards the west, in the compound of the temple, is a small shrine of Patleshvar Mahadev whose liṅga, is seen deep, in the ground. A back door to the west, leads to an open platform from where a fine view of the forest valleys and the green fields of distant plains is obtainable. From Vasishtha-Ashram, the Abu road, is only about 6 or 7 miles but the way is not safe and easy. In the same compound, resting on the eastern wall of the temple, are arranged in one line, some idols of Five Pandavas, Shankar, Harish Chandra, Sheshshayi Vishnu, Janmejaya, Gautam, Ganapati, Vārah Avatar, Surya Narain, Raja Ambarish, Badrinarain, Sarasvati, Anjana etc. Out of these, the idol of Badrinarain, carved out of black stone with the water of the Ganges gushing out from its head and the snake mālā (band) lying in the hands from the backside is the most beautiful. A few of these idols bear the inscriptions of the Thirteenth century. In the north-eastern corner, is a small temple of Ranchod Raiji (Lord Shri Krishna) and a grove of grapes, nearby.

In front of the main shrine and behind the wall of small cells, is to be seen, the Agni-kund—the sacrificial fire-pit of Vasishta Muni from which the Rajput clans, that is, Parmar, Parihar, Solanki (Chaulukyas) and Chouhans, came out.

In the same compound to the extreme south, we find the Ashram of the Hindu monks who provide foodstuffs, utensils etc. to the needy pilgrims. There are also big trees with thick foliage, round about the Ashram which lend good appearance. The Vasistha Ashram, on the whole is quiet and lovely place. Every year a fair is held, on the full moon day of the month of Ashadh (coinciding with the month of August).

Jamadagni Ashram

A further downwards, from Vasishtha-Ashram, at a distance of 2 or 3 miles, on the slopes of the Mount Abu, is Jamadagni Ashram, associated with the ancient Rishi Jamadagni. It is difficult to descend and also there is nothing of special interest.

Gautama Ashram

To the west of Vasishta Ashram, at a distance of about 3 miles, we come to Gautama Ashram, after descending the flight of steps. There is a small shrine dedicated to the sage Gautama, with an image of Vishnu and the images of Rishi Gautama and his wife Ahalyā (mentioned in the Ramayana). The inscription outside the temple, mentions that during the reign of Maharāv Udai Singh, two ladies Parvati and Champa Bai, built the flight of steps in V.S. 1613, Vaisakh Shukla 3.

Madhava Ashram

About five miles down the slope from Vasishtha Ashram, is Madhava Ashram. The descent to this Ashram and Gautama Ashram is difficult and the visitors are advised not to come alone.

THE SLOPES

Vashthanji

On the northern slope of Abu, towards Guru Shikar,

there is a village called Sher, at a distance of 10 to 12 miles. This is a beautiful and lovely place, in the lap of the mother nature. There is a big cave 18 ft. long, 12 ft. broad and 6 ft. high in which is enshrined a marble image of Vishnu with his ten incarnations. Besides, there are images of Shiva linga, Parvati, Ganesh and Garuda. The image of Garuda (Eagle) is very fine, made of black marble stone, and it is mounted on Sheshnag. Outside the temple, are the figures of Ganesh, Boar incarnation, Bhairava, Brahmā and others. This place is famous as Vashthanji, the corrupt form of Vatsyanji, visited every year, by thousands of pilgrims from the nearby places. The descent from the mount, would be difficult and the convenient way could be from Isari village, which is to the north of a village Shergaon in the Sirohi district and about two miles from the foot of Abu.

Suraj-Kund

Half way between Vasthanji and Shergaon, is Suraj Kund where the water is collected in a curious stone and remains filled up throughout the year.

The sacred places near Utraj

There are a few places of sanctity, in the vicinity of Utraj, a village of Abu, on the other side of Guru Shikar. They are Kedarnath Mahadev, Mataganji goddess, Panchdevala Mahadev, Badrinath Temple, Khadepuri Baba's Gupha; Pandava Gupha and Ganeshji.

Baylay's walk

A road from the Jaipur House on Mount Abu, extends to about three miles and is named after Col. Baylay of the former Political Department. The walk is very pleasant and presents a beautiful view of the plains in front f Mount Abu.

Palanpur point

At a distance of about 2 miles from Sirohi Kothī (Abu camp area) after climbing the hill, we come to a small hill from which the town of Palanpur is visible. This is why it is called Palanpur point. It is not a place of any further interest for the visitors.

Devāngan and Krodidhaj

Descending two miles from the sunset point, a beaten track leads to Devāngan or 'Court of the Gods'', at some height. It is situated, surrounded by bamboo and other magnificent trees. It is an ancient place. According to the traditions, there was an ancient city by the name of Lakhavati. The traces of its ancient glory are found in its remnants of bricks and old images which provide an ample scope for investigators, archaeologists and the students of history. In the old shrıne of Devānganji, there is a huge image of the God Visnu, and some more of it (God Vishnu) are lying in the courtyard in Narshiṁha and Buddha forms, besides the sculptures of few goddesses. The Vishnu in Buddha form, is shown sitting, in the padmāsana, with two arms placed in Dhyanamudra (meditating pose) and the two upper ones carıying the conch and the lotus. Besides, on the other side of the stream, there is a big Trimurti of Lord Shiva, fixed on the wall of a deserted temple. It is finely carved image belonging to the 11th century. Some of the beautiful idols, have been shifted to State Museum in Raj Bhavan, inaugurated by Dr. Sampurnanand, the former Governor of Rajasthan, in the month of December 1965. In State Museum, there is a fine display of articles of antiquity including the penpictures.

Krodidhaj

At a distance of about a mile, there is the famous

temple of Krodidhaj dedicated to the Sun-God, having a black stone image of the sun being worshipped. The temple seems to be older than the image. Outside the Sabhamandap of the temple, there is another smaller shrine of the Sun God. Near the entrance of this temple, is preserved a big marble sculpture of the Sun, partly mutilated which seems to have been installed initially. On one of the pillars of the Sabhamandap, is carved the disc (chakra) of the sun, while on two others are inscriptions of V.S. 1204. There are more shrines in the area with images of goddesses and Sun. The shrine of Surya, is in dilapidated condition and sculptures of Surya, Sheshnag, Narain, Vishnu, Hara—Gauri, and others are there. Every year, on the full moon of Shravana, a *mela* is held. From Krodidhaj, Anādra village is at a distance of about 2½ miles.

DELWADA ANĀDRA ROUTE

Anādra Gate or Abu gate or Anādra Point

From Delwada, at a distance of about two miles, by the main road via Limbdi Kothi and Nakhi Lake and about a mile from Abu camp (Mount Abu) we come down to Abu gate, Anādra Taleti and Anādra village. A huge rock, standing at this point, has been given the name of Abu Gate or Anādra Gate and this is also called Anādra Point. To the right of Abu Gate, there is the small shrine of Ganapati, on a small hill where the residents of Mount Abu visit it on the Ganesh Chaturthi day (Bhādrapada Shukla 4) and at a little height from the Ganesh temple, is a cave by the name of Craig Point or Gurugupha.

Anādra Taleti

The descent from the Abu Gate to Anadra Taleti is about 3 miles. Walking about half a mile, we reach Amba-

Pani or Ambavadiand still downwards, there is a drinking watershed, maintained in summer by Modi Masudilal. The place, is very lovely and cool, surrounded by trees on all sides. At taleti, there is an arrangement for a free supply of both hot (boiled) and cold water and a drinking water shed (called Parva in Gujarati and *Piao* in Hindi) is maintained throughout the year excepting the rainy season by the Jain Svetamber Karkhana, Delwada.

Anādra village

From Anadra Taleti, at a distance of nearly 2 miles, a Kacha road, leads to the old village of Anādra. It is also mentioned as Handaudra in incriptions and Hanadra or Hadadru in literary works. There were formerly many Jain families and temples here. There still exists a big old temple of Shri Adeshvar recently repaired and there are two Upāsarās (rest houses of Jain monks) and a Dharmashālā for the Jain pilgrims. There is a public rest house, a post office and a temple of the Sun-god.

ABU ROAD

After visiting various places of interest and importance on the hill, we take the downward journey to Abu Road.

Ārna Taleti

On the road to Abu Road, from Mount Abu, near the mile stone No. 4-2, is the village of Ārna. Being situated on the low level, it is called Arna Taleti. There is a Jain Dharmashala and a Jain small shrine in which is worshipped a chovisi metal image. The facilities are provided to Jain monks, Jain Laymenand lay women, passing by this route, in the form of hot (boiled) and cold water. The Dharmashala is under the management of Achalgarh Jain Karkhana.

Sat-Ghuma or Sapta-Ghuma

Near mile stone no. 9, the road goes winding up, on one side of the mountain like a spiral stair, taking seven turns one after the other. On the side of the rock, it presents a beautiful sight of the deep valley, with its thick growth of wild trees and the noisy streams, falling in the rainy season. It ends at mile-stone no 7. Due to the zig-zag way and seven turnings, it is called Sapta-Ghuma.

Shanti Ashram

On the left hand side, near the milestone, 13-2, on a high altitude, is situated, a 'Shanti Ashram' built by the Svetamber Jain community at the behest of the well-known Jain Yogi Shri Shanti Suriji. This is a double—storeyed building, with a few quarters for the pilgrims who want to stay there and the necessary facilities in the form of beds, utensils, boiled water etc, are provided. There are also separate quarters for monks of other sects. It is open for all communities.

Hrishi-Kesha

About a mile and a half from Shanti Ashram (mile stone (13-2) is the shrine of Hrishikesh, approachable by a difficult route. This is a famous temple of Vishnu, known as Hrishikesh, situated at the foot of Mount Abu and built by king Ambarisha of Amaravati. It is also said that Lord Krishna, on his way to Mathura, encamped here for sometimes. There is a monastery, dharmashala, kund, and a temple of Shiva. On the back side of it is a beautiful platform where Puranic King, Ambarisha used to meditate. It is said that they are the ruins of the ancient Amaravati. It has a charming natural scenery.

Jvala-devi cave and Ruined Jain Shrines

To the west of Shanti Ashrama on a rock, is Jvala-devi cave in which goddess Jvaladevi is worshipped. She has four hands and a pig is shown as her vehicle. She is regarded as the sister of goddess Adhardevi. It is believed that a subterranean passage from this cave leads to the shrine of Adhardevi. Near the cave, are lying gateways of some Jain temples, in ruins. Just stepping downwards from the cave, to its south are two ruined brick structures which are believed to be of Jain temples because one of them is dedicated to the Tirthankar Chandraprabhu whose Yakshini is known as Jvaladevi.

Tower of Silence

Near the milestone 15, at a short distance from the main road, is the Tower of Silence which was built by Parsi gentleman, by the name of Motabhai Bhikaji, for performing the last rites of a Zoroastrian.

Manpur Jain temple

Near the milestone no. 16, at a distance of about two furlongs, on the way to Hrshikesha, there is the village of Mānpur, where there is an old temple in ruins. In the temple of there is a mutilated image, Rikhabdev with an inscription of the year 1507 V.S. It has a sanctuary, Gudha-mandap, a chowki, in front, with a bhramti and the compound wall. Also, there are signs, of dharma-shala, a small garden and a few fields, all properties of this temple.

Bhadrakali and Umbarani

On the way to Hrisikesha, there is Bhadrakali temple rebuilt and consecrated in V.S. 1979 by Maharav Kesar Sinha ex-ruler of the old Sirohi State. Near about this temple, are the ruins of a Jain shrine, to the left of a Nala. Also about half a mile from Bhadrakali temple, is umbarani, an old village which has been called as uvarani, in an inscription of V.S. 1287 in Luna-Vasahi temple of Delwada. It was a much bigger place with good many Jain shrines. This place is required to be explored by archaeologists.

Kharādi—Abu Road

The last terminus of our journey is Abu-Road, which is also called Kharādi; situated on the Banas river. This is an important town. In the town, is a Jain Dharmshala managed, by Anandji Kalyanji Pedhi, Ahmedabad, for Jain pilgrims. There is a Jain shrine also in it. Opposite to it, there is Jain Digamber Dharamshala, a Digamber Jain Shrine and a big Dharmshala for the Hindus. From Abu Road Bus stand, the S.T.C. buses, run to Ambaji—the celebrated shrine of goddess Ambika, the full reference of which has been given in Appendix. I.

Appendix I

AMBAJI

About 14 miles south-west of Abu Road, is a famous temple of Ambaji, well-known in Gujarat and Rajasthan. The Goddess Ambaji is also known as Ārāsoori, the name derived from the hill Ārāssor, in close proximity of the temple. The shrine of Ambaji, is very old but majestic. There is no idol of the goddess as we find one in Vimal Vasahi at Abu. It is said that depiction of the goddess Ambaji has been decorated by fine ornaments and rich clothes. The temple was constructed mostly with the marble stones which are found in abundance.

Though the temple is very old one yet no historical references are available. There are, however, some inscriptions of the 17the century but they do not afford any historical data of its antiquity. It is for the archaeologists and the historians, to explore this region which lies in Gujarat.

The people from far and wide, come to visit the temple in large numbers and offer gifts, in the forms of coconuts, sweets and ready-made garments, for the Devi (goddess), in fulfilment of their worldly desires, at the invocation of Ambaji. These presentations, are offered, before the deity when the doorway of the temple, is open, at fixed hours. Before this, pilgrims crowd the outer portions of the temple including the staircase. On every full moon day (Purnima), in a month, there is extra-ordinary rush of the pilgrims. But on two occasions, that is, the full moon days of Ashvina and Chaitra months, there are big congregations of the visitors when the *mela* is held.

From Abu Road, the Rajasthan S.T.C. buses ply every day, regularly, and from Palanpur, Ahmedabad, and Tārangaji from the Gujarat side. Many Dharmashalas, have been constructed, in close vicinity of the temple, for the comfort of pilgrims. The visitors have to pay per head some pilgrim-tax to the village Panchayat Ambaji.

Appendix II

CHANDRAVATI

The ancient capital city, Chandravati, now lying in ruins, is about four miles to the south-west of Abu Road. Chandravati, is familiar word in many Jain works. It is well known in Rajasthan and Gujarat. The old city, with ruined Jain and Shiva temples and crumbling edifices and monuments, speaks of its past glory. It has its flourishing trade, art and architecture as well as its civilisation and culture. The historic traditions of its brave and chivalrous heroes, are writ large on the old monuments. In the Jain writings of the fifteenth century, it has been mentioned that at that time, there existed 444 Jain and 999 Shiva temples, in Chandravati. It is therefore no wonder if this place remained grand and glorious, in the old days. The remains of the capital city, are found spread over, from 'Toda Gate' to Maval Ry. station. The city was devastated, by successive invasions of Muslim fanatics and iconoclasts. Today, it is a deserted place, covered with the debris of the tottered buildings, pillars and carved domes. Being in plains, it has not found a safe place against the foreign onslaughts and its inhabitants sought refuge, in surrounding secure places, in the Aravalli hills or near about them. When Col. Tod visited this place in 1882 A.D., it was in a desolated condition.

For exploring its antiquity, we have to search for the ancient Jain texts in which large references are given. Acharya Svayamprabha Suri, the fifth pontiff of Lord Parashva Nath, living in the fourth century B.C. had great influence, in the region round about Chandravati. He converted many Rajputs including some princes, into Jainism. Shrimal—Nagar (modern Bhinmal) was the capital of Raja Jai Sen of the Surya (Sun) dynasty and he adopted Jain religion with 90,000 families. He had two sons, namely Bhimsen and Chandra Sen. The former was the follower of Brahmin cult and he remained at Bhinmal. His younger brother, Chandra Sen, migrated from Bhinmal and founded the city of Chandravati, after his name, near about 4th Century B.C. and ruled over it. He was a great follower of Jain religion. There lived many millionaires and multimillionaires who were mostly Jains. They spent lacs of rupees, in construction of the rich and artistic Jain temples. 79 years before Vikram Samvat (V.S.), a grand temple of Lord Mahavir, with fifty-two small shrines was constructed by Shrimal Rāma Shārdūl, at the cost of about 9 lacs of rupees. Between V.S. 521 to V.S. 557, when a great Jain Acharya, Siddha Sen Suri VI, entered the city of Chandravati, Seth Sāngan spent 1½ lacs of rupees, alone for his reception and also installed an idol of Mahavir made of gold, measuring 120 finger-tips. He also built a small shrine in his home in which he placed the idol of Lord Parshva Nath. In this way, he spent nearly one crore of rupees, for religious purposes. It is said that in the days of prosperity of this ancient city, there were hundreds of Jain temples and lacs of their worshippers. Madan, the son of Yashovir, of Porwal community and the minister of Rao Sajjan Sen, laid down a beautiful garden in which he built an attractive shrine of Lord Mahavir. In the beginning of the seventh century V.S., the Jains of this city were so rich and generous, that 360 multi-millionaires, used to give feasts every day, turn by turn throughout the year, (according to Hindu calendar, there are 360 days in a year) so no necessity could arise, to light fire in one's hearth and home. Any Jain, coming to this city, was offered one gold mohur and one gold brick, to start his business. This instance points to the mutual help, and sympathy, shown towards one's co-religionists, in those days.[1]

Chandravati, also remained the Capital of Parmars and Deora kings. It was only in 1405 A.D. that Rao Sheshmal Deora Chauhan Chief, shifted his capital from Chadravati to Sirohi. The latest reference of Chandravati, is found in Jain chronicles, upto 1689 A.D. Thus we find that the prosperity of Chandravati, lasted from the ancient times upto the fifteenth century. It is, therefore, no wonder that the boundaries of Chandravati, extended upto 18 miles. It was also an important centre of trade and commerce. The Silks and calicoes of Ahmedabad,* owed most of their fame, to the skill of Chandravati weavers and dyers. The old coins discovered here, prove the fact that it was also a place of international trade.

There is a great scope for further investigation into the past glories of Chandravati which lies still hidden in its heaps of stones and sculptures, Col. Tod describes the present desolate condition of Chandravati, in these words.

"Nature herself, so prolific in these regions, is rapidly covering the glories of the Parmar with an impenetrable veil. The silence of the desolation reigns among these magnificent shrines and the once populous streets which religion and commerce united to feel with wealthy votaries, are now occupied by the tiger and the bear or the scarcely more civilized Bhil."

1. Muni Gyān Sunder; Bhagavan Parshva Nath Ki Parampara Itihasa pp. 1027-1029.

APPENDIX III

KUMBHARIYAJI[1]

Resembling in many respects with the Delwada Jain temples of Abu and sometimes more beautiful and artistic, are the Jain shrines of Kumbhariyaji, situated at a distance of 16 miles from Abu Road and about 2 miles from Ambaji. It, is situated on the bus-route to Palanpur. Its ancient name was Kunti-nagari as mentioned in Jain texts. There, existed once 300 temples in the period between V.S. 370 and V.S. 400. At present, there are only five Jain temples with excellent carvings and high sanctuaries, managed by Anandji Kalyanji Pedhi, Ahmedabad. It is still not known who built these temples, but the inscriptions found here, lead us to believe that they were constructed in the 11th century A.D., the oldest inscription, being from V.S. 1118 (1061 A.D.).[2] There are as many as 38 inscriptions deciphered by Muni Jayant Vijayaji, in his book 'Arbudachal Pradakhsina Jain Lekh Samdoh'. In the oldest inscription, it was also called 'Ārāsana.'

The ancient temples of Kumbhariyaji, are in the Danta taluka of Banas-kanta district. They are about one

1. Most of the descriptions, have been taken from the manuscript essay on Kumbhariyaji, written in Gujarati, by Shri Chandulal Lallu Bhai Shah of Ahmedabad, the present manager of the Kumbhariyaji Jain temple under the caption.

"प्राचीन जैन तीर्थ कुंभारिया जी"

2. The inscription reads as follows :

"ॐ ।। संवत् 1118 फागुन सुदी 9 सोमे । आरासणाभिधाने स्थाने तीर्थाधिपस्य प्रतिमा कारिता..........."

thousand years old. From Gujarat side, they are 42 miles from Palanpur and 35 miles from Khed-brahma. They are also approachable, by S.T. buses from Ambaji. The private cars and taxis also ply, from all sides. It is 1700 ft. above sea-level, surrounded on all sides by the hilly ranges and forests. Its climate, is healthy and excellent. The atmosphere is calm and peaceful, in natural surroundings. There are facilities of lodging and boarding for the Jain pilgrims. There are, in all five temples namely (1) The big temple of Neminath (2) The temple of Mahavir (3) The temple of Parshvanath (4) The temple of Shantinath and (5) The temple of Shambhavanath. The faces as of the chief deities, in all these temples are, to the north and have compound walls. Except in the last temple, there are twenty-four small shrines in each of other four temples. All the temples, from top to bottom are built of the marble stones.

The Neminath temple

This temple is the biggest, highest and the most extensive of all. The outer part of the sanctuary, is handsome and artistic, carved with big and beautiful figures of gods and goddesses, yaksās and yakshinis, all round the circumbulatory passage, with the band of elephants, below it. On entering the main doorway of the temple, we catch the glimpse of the idol of Lord Neminath, the chief deity. The temple consists of Shrinagar Chowki, Ranga-mandap, and Sabha-mandap. In the main sanctum, the idol of Neminath, is attractive and impressive. Outside the main sanctum, are two big sculptures of standing Jinas (kaussagias), in silent meditation and the similar in the sabhamandap (courtyard) with the addition of fine slab of 170 small Jinas. In the central dome of Rang-mandap, are carved out, the fourteen dreams (seen, by the mother of the would—be Tirthankar when he or she comes in his or her mother's womb), reliefs of eight auspicious signs and, the figures of gods and goddesses and Vidya devis (goddesses of knowledge.)

In the temple, we see the inscriptions of marble stones, dating from V.S. 1214 to V.S. 1675. It appears that this shrine was built near about V.S. 1174 (1117 A.D.), by the minister Pāsil of Ārāsan, the old name of Kumbhariya village. It was damaged by Allaudin Khilji when his forces attacked it, in about V.S. 1356. After that, it was repaired and the second consecration ceremony took place, on Magh Shukla 4 V.S. 1675, at the hands of Bhattārak Shri Vijaidev Suri, Pandit Kushalsagar Suri and their pupils, during the times of the famous Acharya Hīr Vijaya Suri.

The Mahavir Svami temple.

In the main shrine, there is the idol of Mahavir Svami. The carvings of the temple are superior to the other temples, in art, workmanship and construction. One is taken by surprise, to look at its grandeur and unique sculpture which can easily be compared with that of the Delwara temples at mount Abu. On the pedestal, there is an inscription of V.S. 1128 from which it can be safely concluded that this shrine was built some 900 years before. On the pillars of the temple, are engraved the beautiful figures of gods, goddesses, in handsome dancing poses. Inside the dome, there is wonderful detailed carving.

On all sides of the pillars, there are ceilings, with seven panels, on each side. On one panel is seen the Jain Tirthankar in the lap of his mother, in the form of a child. On the second panel, there are the Jain images of the present chovisi and on other panels are depicted the scenes from the life of Lord Parshvanath—the fourteen dreams seen by his mother, uplifting of the lord by Indra, on Meru mountain, and his other events of life including tormentation by Kamath Rishi. The temple was destroyed by Muslim invasions and was later repaired and consecrated in V.S. 1675.

The Parshvanath temple

It is, also a grand temple with splendid sculpture. It consists of Chowkis, Rangmandap, Sabhamadap and the main sanctum. The idol of Lord Parshvanath is enshrined, in the main shrine. In the sabhamandap, there are the figures of two big Kaussagias, on the pedestal of which are inscriptions of 1176 V.S. In this shrine, there are fine carvings on the four pillars of Sabhamandap, torans (arches). The doors and the domes have also been artistically carved out in V.S. 1675. This temple was consecrated in V.S. 1675.

The Shantinath temple

The sculptures, the arrangement of the pillars, torans and ceilings, are similar to those in the Mahavir Svami temple. The idols, in many small shrines of the temple, were installed on Ashadh Sud 2, V.S. 1087 as indicated by the inscriptions of the temple. Besides there are found the old inscriptions of V.S. 1110 and V.S. 1138. From this it seems that this temple was built, first of all the temples of Kumbhariyaji.

The Shambhavanath temple

It is situated, at some distance from the other temples. It is a small but beautiful shrine. No inscription has been found about its builder. It appears that this temple was built by a rich person of this place. From the appearance of the temple, it may be inferred that it is nearly 1000 years old, when the small town of Ārāsan and the rich city of Chandravati, were prospering. The Solanki kings ruled over Gujarat, in those days and the administration of these places was carried on by the Jain ministers.

It may be concluded that these famous temples might have been built by the ministers of Gujarat—Vimal Shah, Goga and Pasil, the work might have been commenced from V.S. 1080. The small cells and Rangmandaps, were constructed, later on, from time to time, in different periods. As already mentioned these temples were destroyed by Allauddin Khilji and looked deserted, till later repairs were done in V.S. 1675. These temples, being desolated and situated in the jungles could not gain much importance. Since the management of the temples, came into the hands of Anandji Kalyanji Pedhi, they are gradually growing in importance. With good publicity, they can now stand in line with the Delwada Jain temples of Abu.[1]

1. The detailed account of Kumbhariyaji can be read from the Gujarati book, Shri Kumbhariyaji or Arasan Tirth Mala, published by Yasovijaya Jain Granth Mala, Gandhi Chowk Bhavanagar.

APPENDIX IV

MUNGTHALĀ

At a distance of—4½ miles from Abu Road, on the road going to Mandar, there is a small village of Mungthalā. It is famous for Shiva shrine and the old Jain temple of Lord Mahavir. Both the places are ancient and have historical importance.

The shrine of Shiva is known by the name of Shri Mudgaleshvar Mahadev where is found a very old inscription of the year 895 A.D. In the temple of Shri Mahavir Svami, there is an inscription of 1159 A.D. and the other inscriptions of the 13th, 14th, 15th and 16th centuries. The inscription of 1159 A.D., is very important as it reveals that Lord Mahavir when he was a recluse, came over to this place, in the thirty-seventh year of his life.[1] This fact finds support from some of the contemporary, Jain writings of the later middle ages. This is the reason why Mungthala is known as Mahātīrth Mungthalā.

There is need for further research into the antiquity of this spot which contains both Shaiva and Jain monu-

1. The inscription is engraved upon the pillar, on the right side of the chowki, and dates from V. S. 1216 Vaisakh Vadi 5, Monday It reads as follows.

"पूर्वे छद्मस्थ कालेऽर्बुदभुवि यमिनः कुर्वतः सद्विहारं,
(सप्त) त्रिंशे च वर्षे वहति भगवतो जन्मतः कारिता स्ता (सा)
श्री देवार्यस्य यस्योल्लसदुपलमयी पूर्णराजेन राज्ञा,
श्री केशी सु (शिना) प्रतिप्ठः स जयति हि जिनस्तीर्थमुंडस्थलस्तु ॥

There is also a popular saying as under :—

नाणा दियाना अने नादिया, जीवितस्वामी वांदिया"

ments of the old times. It is also maintained that Lord Mahavir, came to Bamanvadji where the pointed wooden nails hammered into the ears of Mahavir in meditation, were takens out, at this place. Mahavir visited Mount Abu while leading the life of a monk. There is a popular belief among the Jains that the temples of Nānā, Diyānā and Nadia, were constructed, during, the life time of Mahavir Svami.

Therefore, a link has to be established by the historians and archaeologists, about Mahavir's travels, towards Abu region after excavations and exploration, which might lead to a big discovery in the field of ancient history of India.

Appendix V

BĀMANVĀDJI

Bāmanvādji, is 45 miles from Mount Abu, 27 miles from Abu Road 5 miles from Sirohi Road. It is an old place of pilgrimage, managed by Seth Kalyanji Parmanandji Pedhi, Sirohi. The temple is said to have been built by the emperor Samprati, some 2,100 years before. It is believed that Lord Mahavir, when he was an ascetic visited this place and the wooden nails, hammered into his ears were taken out there. The footprints of Mahavir, are found here and the actual place of taking out the nails, is believed to be there. In 764 A.D., the renovation ceremony of the temple took place and the temple was built long before it. In the 10th century, new cells were erected round the main sanctum. The inscriptions of V.S. 1519 are found in most of the cells. The idol of Lord Mahavir is made of sand particles and such idols are very scarcely found. The pearl plaster has also been rubbed, on the idol from time to time. There are outside the main temples, painted marble Pattas (slabs), covered with glasses, depicting the scenes from the twenty-seven past lives of Mahavir, on the both sides of the main door.

Near the temple, there is a *chattri*, with the footprints of Lord Mahavir, on the top of the hill. Close to the *chattri*, is fine bungalow where the famous Yogiraj Shri Shanti Suriji, used to meditate when he was alive. Around the hill, the construction work is going on, according to the plan of famous Sammet Shikar Tirth. This temple is visited with reverence, by all classes of people including Bhils and Garasias. The Jains consider it as a great place of pilgrimage and visit in large numbers. The ex-ruler of Sirohi, also used to visit the place and they offered certain land and wells, for the maintenance of the temple. There is a Dharmashala, a Bhojanshala for the Jains.

There are 23 inscriptions in all in Bamanvadji, the oldest dating from V.S. 1349 (1292 A.D.)[1] and the latest dating from V.S. 1876 (1819 A.D.) which relates about some land gifted to the temple of Bamanvadji by the ex-ruler of Sirohi Maharav Shiva Sinha.

1. The oldest inscription reads as follows :—
"सं० 1349 ज्येष्ठ सु० 10 श्री दुस्माधान्वये महं हरिराजपुत्रेण समरसिंहेन स्वपितामहीमहं हासलदेविश्रेयसे श्रीपार्श्वनाथबिंबं कारितं—बृहद्गच्छे श्रीमुनिरत्नसूरिभिः ॥

Appendix VI

NĀDIA

Nearly three miles from Bamanvadji is a village of Nadia. Dhanāshah who built the renowned temple of Ranakpur, was the resident of this place. It is also known by the name of Nandipur. There are two noteworthy places. The first is the place where there is engraved on stone, a figure of the serpent Chandkaushik who had bitten the body of Lord Mahavir with his poisonous teeth, when he was an ascetic. On biting, the white blood, oozed out of the body of the Lord—expression of universal love towards all creatures of the world. There are few old writings on the *chattris* of Chandkoushik which are not readable. These monuments lead us to believe that Lord Mahavir, must have travelled in Abu Region.

Another place is the temple of Mahavir Svami, near a banian tree. The idol of Mahavir, is unique as it has been hewn from one stone, with its parikar. There are found mostly the inscriptions of 15th century and the oldest is of V.S. 1130 (1073 A.D.)[1]

1. The inscription of V. S. 1130 reads as under.

"संवत् (त्) 1130 वैसाष सुदि 13 नंदियक चैत्यहा (ह) र वापी निर्मापिता सिवगणे (न)"

The above lines are inscribed in the stone slab of the Chowki of water cistern, outside Shrinagar Chowki in the ancient temple of Mahavir Svami.

APPENDIX VII

MIRPUR

Mirpur is at a distance of 10 miles from Sirohi. Its ancient name is Hamirgadh which was a big fort with huge fortification all round it. Now, we see only the remnants of stony walls. Some say that Hamirgadh was founded in 751 A.D. but there is no reliable historical basis for it.

Today, we find four Jain temples, on Dharmashala and a garden. Out of these four temples, only one temple, has an idol inside it and the rest are without idols. The temple is very exquisite and artistic. Many of the carvings are similar, in design, to those in the Delwada temples of Abu. There are some different specimens as well. The domes, the pillars and the borders, are very fine and are rarely found, at other places. There are a few inscriptions in the temple of the sixteenth century which proves the existence of Hamirgadh in this century. There is an inscription of V.S. 1219 (1162 A.D.) in the temple which is the oldest and it throws some light on the history of Hamirgah.[1]

There are eight more inscriptions out of which seven date from the 12th to 15th centuries while the latest is of V.S. 1903 (19th century A.D.) which relates to the land gifted by the Thakur of Nadia.

1. The inscription reads as follows :—

"संवत्: 1219 आषाढ़ सुदि 10 रवौ श्रे·········चतुर्विंशति (:) कारिता प्रतिष्ठिता श्रीचन्द्रसिंह सूरिभिः ॥

Mirpur, lies on the *pucca* road, from Sirohi to Anādra. There is a dense forest inhabited by bears, tigers and other animals of the jungle, round about it. The Jain temples are under the management of Seth Kalyanji Parmanandji Pedhi, Sirohi.

Appendix VIII

SIROHI

Sirohi, is 53 miles from Mount Abu, 35 miles from Abu Road and 13 miles from Sirohi Road. It is an ancient city, by the name of Shivapuri, founded by Shivasen, the brother of Jayasen of Shrimālnagar (Bhinmal) near about fourth century B.C. Sirohi, remained the capital of the former Sirohi State since 1405 A.D. when Rao Sheshmal abandoned Chandravati. Swords of Sirohi, were famous and there are few artists who are expert in this art. At present, after the merger of the Sirohi State, in Rajasthan, it is the headquarters of the district.

In all, there are sixteen Jain temples, out of which thirteen, are just in one line. Many temples, are of the 17th century and the temple of Chaumukhji is very magnificent having three storeyes. The shrine was built by Pragvat Singhi Mehajalji and the consecration ceremony was performed, at the hands of Acharya Shri Vijaisen Suri in V.S. 1634 (1577 A.D.). The head-office of the managing committee of Delwada, Bamanvadji and Mirpur and some other temples, is situated here by the name of Seth Kalyanji Parmanandji Pedhi.

There are 34 inscriptions in all the Jain temples, the oldest of them dates from V.S. 1224 (1167 A.D.)

1. The inscription is on the metal, image in the temple of Shri Godi Parshvanath. It reads as follows:—

ॐ ॥ सं (०) 1224 चैत्र वदि 5 व्र (ब्र) ह्माणगच्छे आजड़ श्रेयसे जसदेवेन झय (?) प्रतिमा कारिता ॥"

There are many good Hindu temples, besides the palaces of the ex-ruler of Sirohi state, Rest-houses, a Hospital and the Municipality. There is also a Degree College and one Agriculture College. Two miles from it, is the temple of Sarneshvar Mahadev. The historical figure, Timur lane was cured of paralysis, by the invocation of Lord Shiva there. Two and a half miles from Sarneshvar is a noteworthy fort of Kolargadh. It was a prosperous town, during the reign of Akbar. Many battles were fought there for the defence of Sirohi, by the Sirohi rulers, against the mighty forces of Akbar. The fort is, now in ruins. The great fort and its walls indicate the prosperity which the fort enjoyed in the old days. On the hill, is a temple of Ambeshvar Mahadev where people visit it in good numbers on every monday. We also find there, a Jain temple of Lord Adinath, which is in ruins. Pragvat Singhi Javanmal brought the idol, repaired the temple and also constructed a Dharmashala there. It is a fine place, for enjoyment, meditation and picnic.

Appendix IX

THE VALIANT VIMAL SHAH

Gujarat reached the pinnacle of its glory in the eleventh century. The art and culture spread wide over this region. The rulers and the ministers exhibited supreme courage and bravery and extended the kingdom of Gujarat. The popularity of Jainism spread over the wide area near about Anhilpurpātan which was founded by Vanraj of Chavada dynasty, under the influence of a Jain Acharya Shri Shilaguna Suri and with the help of a Jain named Champa. During this time, Buddhism was gradually vanishing and the influence Brahmanism was also diminishing. Jainism became more or less a popular religion in Gujarat. A few kings of Gujarat, adopted Jainism as their main religion. Vimal, Munjāl, Udayana and Vastupal Tejpal all ministers of Gujarat were the chief followers of Jain religion. They rendered great services to enhance the glory of Gujarat. The Jain Acharyas-Suracharya, Vardhaman Suri and Hem Chandracharya, preached the principles of *Ahimsa* (Nonviolence), to the common people.

Under such circumstances prevailing in Gujarat, a fearless and chivalrous man—Vimal Shah—was born and brought up there.

As already stated, Anhilpur, the capital of Gujarat, was established by Vanraj in the year 802 V.S. (745 A.D.) and the Jains of the neighbouring region began to settle there. Many people migrated from Shrimalnagar (Bhinmal). Among them was Nināg. The ancestor of Vimal Shah who first settled in Gambhu village and then moved to Pāttan, during the reign of Vanraj. Lāhir, the son of

Ninag, was very brave and courageous. He was appointed the commander-in-chief of Gujarat. In the pedigree of Lāhir, came Vir who was the General of the king Durlabhraj of Gujarat. Vir was the father of Vimal Shah who renounced the world when Vimal was only a lad of fifteen. In his student life, he was very intelligent, clever and self-respecting boy. When he played in the streets and rode on the horse-back, the people were attracted towards him to look at his unsurpassed beauty. Before renunciation, his father gave the advice, not to tolerate injustice, to keep away from all kinds of sin, to perform the meritorious deeds and to obey the words of the Tirthankar. So instructed and inspired by the words of his father, he was imbued with the spirit of justice, righteousness and chivalry. So smart and sublime was he that the ministers of Pātan looked him with an eye of jealousy.

Once, when Vimal was riding on a horse, he came across a group of ladies belonging to the respectable families who scattered away, here and there in the street due to the swiftness of the horse. The incident reached the ears of the minister Dāmodar who called the boy and rebuked him at his impetuosity. Vimal replied with straight-forwardness that it was no fault of his. He could not control the horse, in spite of his best efforts. Even if the Maharaj would call him, he would tell him the real truth. Vir Mati, the mother of Vimal was a far-sighted lady. She left Pātan, with his two sons, for a village, some 24 miles from Pātan and lived with her brother whose financial position was weak. Both the brothers passed their lives happily together, practising archery, grazing the cattle and ploughing the fields of their maternal-uncle. Both Vimal and his elder brother Nedha, became stout, strong and energetic, by living in the open air, taking pure milk and ghee of the cows and buffaloes. Vimal was very handsome and the villagers, were very much enamoured to see his face. Ambika, a daughter of a bard (chāran) was so much charmed towards him, that one day she entreated Vimal, for love when she came to his house, Vimal could not tolerate this and rebuked her. She felt ashamed and admired his spotless character. Even she blessed him that Ambika, the goddess of Ārāsoor, would help in his future endeavours. Our hero, in his childhood, was noble, fearless and truthful. He was strong in character. The coquettish look of the beautiful Ambika, the daughter of a bard, could not swerve him, from his path.

Then came a proposal for the marriage of Vimal with Shridattā—a beautiful and meritorious daughter of Shridattā, a rich citizen of Pātan. Although the financial condition of Vimal was not good, still Shrichandra, the brother of Shridatta was bent upon this match, knowing the qualities of head and heart of Vimal from his boyhood when they were together in school. Fortunately, Vimal saw something shining in a big hole of a field, when passing out and on digging it, found a vessel full of gold mohurs which he entrusted to his mother.

Later on, Vimal returned to Patan with his mother and brother. His marriage took place with great pomp and show. They passed their lives very happily. In his youth, Vimal gained rich laurels from the king Bhimdev of Gujarat. He won distinction in the festival of heroes, on the banks of Durlabh Tank, where gathered the heroes and the wrestlers. A competition in archery was held in which Vimal and only Vimal blind-folded, could shoot with his arrow, a bird sitting on the branch of a tree. He pierced through a particular petal out of eight petals, piled one upon the other, on the stomach of a lying child, and also struck out the moving earing of a young woman churning the butter-milk. No one assembled could perform such marvellous feats and every one present in the festival, was wonder-struck at the extraordinary skill of this young man. The people gathered there, cheered and applauded him loudly. The king was so much pleased that he made Vimal Shah the commander-in-chief of the Gujarat forces and took his elder brother Nedha, in the council of his advisors.

When Hamir Sumana was ruling over Sindh, he challenged Bhimdeva, the king of Gujarat. The Gujarat army advanced towards Sindh under the able command of Vimalshah. The river Sindhu (Indus) was spanned by the army and the furious battle was waged. At first, the armed forces of Bhimdeva retreated but after the tumultuous battle and the duel between Bhimdeva and Hamir, the Gujarat army came out victorious. The hands of Hamir were chopped off and he fell headlong on the battle-ground. On return, the independent Chedi kingdom, was also won over by Vimal shah. The victory in these wars, established the fame of Vimal and his name spread far and wide. The king Bhimdeva, was also very much pleased at his bravery and gallantry.

The courtiers of Bhimdev grew jealous, to hear about Vimal's powers and skill, in the battle-field. They began to lay trap and to poison the ears of the king Bhimdev, to belittle his prestige. Once, they let loose the lion in the city and Vimal was asked by the king to control him and to put the furious lion into its cage. Vimal had to grapple strong to catch the lion. At one time, he felt as if he was in the clutches of death. But taking courage, he took his dagger, from his waist and piercing it in its mouth, by one hand, caught hold of him by the other. On the exhibition of such marvellous feats, the king presented to him gold-hilted sword and gold-laced dress. Then a duel was arranged between a wrestler and Vimal in which also Vimal came out victorious. All the plans being foiled, the last device was thought upon. The debt of fifty-six lac Tanka was shown, in the books of the State Treasury since the time of his forefather Lahar: Vimal grew angry to hear about such a false charge and he left Pāttan for Chandravati, at the command of Bhimdev, to subdue the king Dhundhuk. He captured Chandravati, without any bloodshed and called himself the Governor of the king of Gujarat.

Vimal began to beautify the city of Chandravati, by constructing fine roads, with shady trees on both the sides, cool reservoirs and wide streets. Attaining the zenith of his military power and worldly prosperity, Vimal, now, thought upon the purification of his soul. His mind gradually, began to detract from the worldly attainments and to search for the inner peace. He brought back Dhundhuk and made him the feudatory of the king Bhimdev. Once upon a time, a great Acharya, Dharmaghosa Suri, visited Chandravati and he was so much influenced by his instruction that he pondered to repent upon his past actions in the battlefields and requested the Acharya, for their atonement. The Suri, instructed him to revive the ancient glory and grandeur of Abu Tirth, by constructing a fine temple over Abu hill, by which his past sins would be expiated, with the washing away of the sins of the pilgrims to this holy temple.

Vimal sought the permission of Bhimdev, purchased land from local Brahmins, by giving them gold mohurs rectangular in shape, equivalent to the space required for the temple premises and made a search for skilled architects. There were famous architects near about Badnagar, in Gujarat and Vimal once himself went to the village of a famous architect, in order to convince that artist that he would like to construct such a matchless temple in the universe which would remain unparalleled in art and craftsmanship. With the ample wealth and resources, provided, by Vimal Shah, marvellous and monumental Mandir (temple) was built by 1500 skilled masons and 1200 labourers, within a period of fourteen years.

Vimal was generous like Karṇa, powerful like Bhima, and an archer like Viswakarmā. He gradually dissociated himself with all the political activities, after creating a heavenly abode, on Arbudgiri. Stones, always drown human beings and do not save them, in a water pool, but this artistic creation of the stones, certainly uplifts them above the surface of the worldly pool. Vimal became disinterested with the worldly affairs and bore no hatred and jealousy. The feelings of truth, non-violence, forgiveness, generosity and charity, found place in his innermost heart. He had no distress or anxiety of any kind in his mind. He and his life-mate—Shridatta, were devoted wholeheartedly to God and the service of mankind. They began to live without any attachment, in the world, just like lotus flowers, though immersed in water but still keeping above its surface. Though not wearing the apparel of a Sādhu, they were monks in real spirit of the term. They were the great citizens of this world. Vimal Shah, is also said to have built a great and artistic temple at Arasoor or Kumbhariyaji, at the base of Mount Abu. It is still in dark where he left his mortal remains. The history does not throw any light on this subject. It must be affirmed that Vimal vanquished vast wealth—a great national heritage to the universe.

APPENDIX X

TWO BIG BROTHERS

Vastupal and Tajpal

Equally important and famous as Vimal Vasahi, is another temple Lunavasahi which also attracts people from far and near. The influence that its sculpture, its calmness and its heavenly beauty cast upon one's mind, lasts not only for this life but also for the lives to come. The carvings wrought in white marble are superb and marvellous. No adequate words can describe them. It was built by the ministers—Vastupal and Tejpal, according to the wishes of Anupamadevi, the wife of Tejpal as Tej Mahal was built by Shahjahan, in the memory of his wife Mumtaz Begum. Its architect was sūtradhār Sobhanadev who demanded gold mohurs to be laid inside the foundation, to test the generosity of the ministers who readily gave them and refused to take them back when they were once dedicated. Within the period of nine years, a unique specimen of sculpture, was erected, by 1500 masons, under the guidance of the architect Sobhandev. The balconies of Sāsu-Bahu and the panel depicting 108 different dancing poses in its ceiling, have been so minutely hewn from the marble stone that they take the breath away from one's heart. The white marble elephants in its Hastishala, have been decorated so beautifully with ornaments, tapestries and ropes that they appear like real white elephants. Besides many artistic designs of flowers, plants, creepers, lotuses, snakes, birds, animals, men and women, gods and goddesses, royal courts, processions, sea-voyages, dances and battlefields, bewitch the visitors and acquaint them with the social, political and commercial trend of those times.

The readers would be curious to know about the lives of the persons who built such a bewildering and a beautiful temple in the world. Such lofty and noble construction emerges only when a man is imbued with the best and the highest feelings in his heart. The Emperor Shahjehan, could create Taj Mahal-one of the seven wonders of the world, actuated by the feelings of love towards his better half but these big brothers, had no such motives except their devotion to the supreme God. Though they were born in the Porwal family of Gujarat, they were the illustrious brothers of the universe. They did not favour any class or creed and liberally donated for the religious and the public cause, from Kedarnath in the north to Kanchi in the south and from Kashi to the Prabhaspattan in the west. They not only built the Jain temples at Palitana, Girnar and Delwada (Abu) but also paid handsome donations of lacs of rupees to Someshwar temple, Kashi Vishwanath temple, Dwarakaji, Prayag, the holy Ganges and Abu. They, even contributed for the construction of the mosques. It is said that they built 3002 Shiva temples 1002 Dharmashalas, 700 Brahmanshalas, 700 lekhashalas or literary institutions, 580 Pinjrapoles (cattle-pounds), 84 big tanks, 484 small reservoirs, 484 step-wells, 32 forts and 700 charity dinner halls besides 84 mosques.

They were also foremost, in the literary field. Whenever they returned from the battlefields, they gave in charity a huge amount to poets and pandits, on auspicious days. They spent some 18 crores of rupees, for getting written Brahamanical and Jain scriptures. They steered the State machinery, with great skill and diplomacy. There was no famine during their times. The subjects were happy, contented and free from the fears of thieves and robbers.

The people followed their respective religions, without any state interference. The tax was imposed according to the rules and regulations. In short, these two big brothers were two great gems of the world. They endeared themselves to the people, with their high efficiency, religious-mindedness, even-handed justice, bold bravery, profound knowledge and sparkling vivacity.

Vastupal Tejpal were the sons of Āsharāj. Their forefathers settled at Patan, in Gujarat in the twelfth century and as ministers, they won laurels and admiration of the Gujaiat kings by their loyalty and sagacity. Vir Somraj, the father of Asharaj, was very trustworthy minister of the famous king Siddharaj Jaisingh. He served the ruler of Gujarat throughout his life with honesty. Asharaj was also the worthy son of the worthy father, inheriting all the good qualities from his father. He was the counsellor of the Gujarat king. The mother of the two brothers, was Kumardevi, the daughter of Abhā who was the minister of Anhilpur. Kumardevi became a widow in the early age but Asharaj married her, on knowing from a Jain monk about the bright future of the sons who would be born from her. The conjugal life was very happy. During those days, the State of Pattan, was not stable. Raja Bhimdav II was brave but arrogant. He attacked the Parmar chief of Abu when he gave his daughter, in marriage to another king. Although, he won the battle but the strength of his forces was weakened. Taking advantage of the internecine feud. Sultan Kutubuddin led his army against Pattan. Many rich and respectable families left Pattan and among them was Asharaj who settled in the village 'Sumhalak' and began to lead a peaceful life. He had four sons and seven daughters. All the four sons were beautiful and bright. The names of the male issues were Luning, Maldev, Vastupal and Tejpal. The daughters were also illustrious as the goddesses and their names were, Jalhu, Malu, Sāu, Dhandevi, Sānā, Vayu and Padamdevi. They had all sort of training from their parents and were highly cultured. The military training was specially imparted, during that time. Among the four sons, Vastupal and Tejpal, were conspicuous, by their sharp intellect, broad vision, chivalry and valour. In the small village of Sumhalak, there was kamal-Vana in the centre of the tank which the lads of the village, tried to reach, by swimming across. None could succeed but the two brothers who had to struggle hard and that too at the peril of their lives. They reached safe the hillock near the Kamalvan, after diving the deep waters and frustrating the attempts of the crocodiles. All the villagers collected at the shore, acclaimed the brave sons of Ashraj, with loud applause.

Bhimdev II had left Pattan and began to live like a Sanyāsi, at a short distance in a jungle. The aged father of Vastupal and Tejpal wanted his sons, to fight against the Muslim king and to re-instate the Solanki king Bhimdev. Bagheda Lavan Parsad, assisted by the twin brothers, entered Pattan and drove out the Śubedar, deputed by Kuttubuddin. At this victory, Lavan Prasad was awarded the title of Mahamandleshwar and the village Dholka and the two brothers were highly honoured.

In the life of a man, three things—ice-covered mountain, vast battlefield and stormy sea, cast a great influence in the mind, at the first sight. Both the brothers were greatly influenced also at first sight of the battlefield. Their father Asharaj died on the way to the Pilgrimage to Shatrunjaya and the elder brother expired prematurely. Both the brothers were in great anxiety and they settled down at Mandli (Mandal) village where they became rich and prosperous. After some time, their elder brother Luning and their mother Kumardevi, also breathed their last.

During that time, Acharya Narchandra Suri came to Patan and instructed the bereaved family of Vastupal and Tejpal, to take a Sangh (congregation) of Jain laymen, laywomen, monks and nuns on the pilgrimage to sha trunjaya (the holy temple at Palitana). When the Sangh proceeded, they met the Rajpurohit someshvardev who introduced them to the king Viradhaval of Dholka. They had talks on the State, social and religious topics. The king was so much impressed by the attractive features, big stature and marked intellect of Vastupal and Tejpal that he took Vastupal as the minister of Khambhat and Dholka and appointed Tejpal as his commander.

Both the brothers passed their time happily as the ministers. They imparted even-handed justice and therefore became popular with the people and the king. The king Viradhaval sent the forces to subdue Chamund—the Saurashtra ruler with whom he had an old enmity under the command of the minister Tejpal. Fierce battle was waged near Bamanthali. Chamund and his brother Sangam were face to face with the Raja Viradhaval and his commander Tejpal. Tejpal saved the life of the king Viradhaval, killed as many soldiers as came in his way and won the battle. The son of Chamund was enthroned and the other feudal kings of Saurashtra were subdued. 10 crores of gold mohurs, 1400 trained horses and 5000 ordinary horses, were gained from this victory. After the conquest of Saurashtra, Tejpal returned to Pattan, visiting holy places of Shatrunjaya, Girnar and Somnath. For the temple of Somnath, the commander Tejpal gifted one lac gold mohurs.

During the ministership of these big brothers, Ghughul was ruling over Godhra. A message was sent to the king by Viradhaval, to pay tribute through his ambassador. Ghughul was brave and stubborn and he sent in reply, a bodice and Kajjal (black eye-ointment), defying the suzerainty of the Gujarat king. A war was immediately declared. Tejpal led the Gujarat forces but at first, the Gujarat army retreated but ultimately, Tejpal himself advanced forward with seven brave Rajputs and upon this the army of Gujarat began to advance. Tejpal made a fatal attack upon Ghughul. He fell down and was made captive. The army of Godhra king scattered away and the king of Godhra was brought to Pattan, in an iron cage. To teach a lesson, Virdhaval ordered that Ghughul should be taken round the city in an iron cage with the very same bodice worn on his body and the eye-ointment, applied to his eyes. But before the execution of his orders, Ghughul committed suicide, in order to evade such blasphemy.

White returning from the battle, Tejpal constructed a big temple of Adinath at Baroda and gave a large amount of money in charity, without any distinction of caste or creed. He also offered valuable presents to Lord Mahadev at Daboi and constructed the Jain temple in Champa gadh and Pavagadh. The king honoured the minister and bestowed 20 villages and the title of 'Sachiva-Chudamani.' upon him.

Both the brothers had broad brows and long hands reaching upto their knees. They were terror to their opponents. They also amused with the poet Someshwar, through his verses. Vastupal himself was a big poet and used to compose poems. They led simple life. Though being Jains, they treated other religions with equanimity. Side by side with the construction of the Jain temple, they also built Hindu Dharmashalas and the Muslim mosques. They always showed compassion towards the poor and the needy and helped them in the best possible manner. They took great interest in education and established many schools in the state. They administered the state so ably that the subjects were happy with their treatment. They were stern on the battleground but kind in their hearts. They took proper care of the wounded soldiers and of the families of the deceased.

When the rejocings were being held over the conquest of Godhra, a message was brought by the ambassador that the king Mauzuddin was marching over Gujarat by the route of Abu hill. Vastupal, himself commanding the army of Gujarat and the feudatory chiefs, met the army of Mauzuddin at the foot of mount Abu, defeated the Muslim army and inflicted a heavy loss. The king Mauzuddin was intending to attack again but in the meanwhile, the wealth of the mother of Mauzuddin while going to Macca, was looted by Chānchyās at Kambhat but the minister Vastupal restored her property, from the Chanchyas. When Mauzuddin came to know about such succour to his mother, he called the minister and wanted to reward him but he refused and only asked for friendship. On this occasion the minister sent five marble stones, to Shatrunjaya for carving out the idols of Adinath. On arrival of Vastupal, at Dhovalakpnr, Rana sent 3 lacs of rupees as an offer which the minister donated in charity. Then he became famous, in the world as a great donor.

At that time, there lived Siddik, a rich merchant in Khambhat fort. One day, he killed his faithful servant, after keeping him hungry and thirsty. The son of the poor servant reached Vastupal and told about the treachrous murder of his father. To avenge such a cruel act, Vastupal himself reached the house of Siddiq who was imprisoned and thrown at the mercy of the sea-waves. When he reached the Gogha port he took the shelter of Shankrāj. Vastupal had to wage a fierce sea-battle in which Siddiq and Shankrāj were killed. In this war, a faithful servant of the minister, exhibited extraordinary skill and courage. He was wounded and ultimately succumbed to the injuries inflicted upon him by the enemy. He was given a rich Jagir and land for the maintenance of family. From the house of Siddiq, many precious stones and riches, came into the hands of the Gujarat ruler. After that Vastupal conquered the coastal region of Maharashtra. Both brothers were so deft in the state adminisration and war tactics that many great heroes trembled before them. Thay had a big army of 1800 bodyguards, 1400 ordinary Rajpu's, 5000 horses 2000 trained horses, 300 milch cows, 2000 ' ullocks and 10,000 armymen. For maintaining such a big regular army, Vastupal spent 4 crores of gold mohur and 4 crores of rupees.

The pilgrimage of the two brothers

Both the brothers were very generous and kind to orphans and crippled persons. When on pilgrimage, they looked whether the Subedars of the newly conqured region, behaved properly or not. They planted trees on the road-sides, constructed step-wells and tanks for drinking water and also built inns, at a short distance, for the comfort of the travellers. They took Sanghas or big congregations to the holy places. Śhatrunjaya and Girnar, were visited with Sanghas, twelve times but the pilgrimages of V. S. 1273, 1285 and 1298 were conspicuous. It is said that there were 36000 Shravakas (Jain laymen), 1900 Seths and Sanghpatis who had the privilege of keeping golden umbrellas on their heads, 24 ivory chariots 50000 bullock-carts, 4505 palanquins, 2200 Sadhus, 1100 Digambar Sadhus, 408 big chariots, 3300 bullock-chariots and 4600 elephants. The number of men and women including servants, approximated to 7 lacs. The sangh pilgrimage was taken under the aegis of Acharya Vijay sen Suri, the family Guru of the minister.

At one time, Vastupal Tejpal, were staying at Hadala village when news of a few dacoits reached them. To keep their wealth safe, they made firm determination to send troops to drive them out. The far-sighted and pious lady, Anupamadevi, the wife of Tejpal, opposed this step to use state power in the religious matter. The money was kept underground and a pit was dug from where a pot full of gold mohurs, came out. Being in possession of great wealth, they constructed a magnificent and marvellous temple at Mount Abu, after the name of their elder brother Luning.

In the meanwhile, the king Viradhaval died and his son Visāldev was installed on the throne of Gujarat. It is said that 182 servants, burnt themselves to death on the pyre of the king Viradhaval. When Vastupal started on the thirteenth pilgrimage, he felt strong feelings of separation from the king Viradhaval and Purohit Someshvar as if his death was near. At last, when he was travelling in Kathiawar, he breathed his last in the village 'Akevāliya', near Limbdi. His brother Tejpal and his son Jayant Singh, were by his side. In spite of the occurrence of such a big calamity, the Sangh proceeded, according to the wishes of Tejpal who cremated his elder brother on the holy land of Shatrunjaya and performed his last rites. A sacred temple was constructed at a place where Vastupal was cremated.

The famous minister Vastupal was so learned that he was awarded 24 titles or honours among them the prominent were 1. Sachiva-Chudamani 2. Sarasvati-Kanthabharana 3. Sarasvati-Dharmaputra 4. Laghu Bhojaraj

5. Datār Chakra Chudamani 6. Chāturya Chāṇakya 7. Gambhir 8. Vir 9. Udār 10. Uttam Nyāya Nipuna. Tejpal also died after 5 years, on the way to the famous Shankheshvar Tirth, feeling the separation of his elder bother—Vastupal. After some time, the pious lady Anupmadevi also expired.

APPENDIX XI

JEERAVALA PARSHVANATH

About 28 miles from Abu road, there is an ancient place of Jain pilgrimage, by the name of Jeeravala Parshvanath. The S.T.C bus runs only upto Revdar, (22 miles from Abu Road) and the rest of the journey is performed in the bus arranged by the temple authorities, from July to March every year. From April to June, the private bus of the temple, starts from Abu Road Jain Dharmshala at 2-30 P.M. and reaches Jeeravala at 4-30 P.M., while the starting time from Jeeravala is 10 A.M. and its arrival at Abu Road is 12 A.M. From Sirohi, there is a regular bus service covering the distance of 40 miles, by direct route. This place is in the Sirohi District of Rajasthan. There is an ancient history attached to this holy place. Jeeravala was also called Jeerāpalli. The idol of Parshvanath was discovered from a cave of near-by village named Kodinar, by Seth Amarasā who saw it in a dream, in the year 200 B.C. (before Vikram. Samvat 143 and Vir Samvat 327). Four years later, it was installed in Jeeravala, in a big temple which took four years to be built. It was repaired after 432 years, that is, in the year 236 A.D. (V.S. 293 and Vir samvat 763), by Jeta shah and Khemashah who led a Sangh (congregation) of 10.000 Jain pilgrims, at the behest of a Jain Acharya, Meru Surishvarji. Next time, it was again repaired in 506 A.D. (V.S. 563 and Vir Samvat 1033) by Seth Hardas, at the instance of Jain Acharya Sahajānand Suriji. There were 1800 Jain families living once in Jeeravala. A Visnu temple was destroyed and desecrated in Jeeravala, by Muslims with the blood and flesh of cows whom they killed. They entered this Jain temple also but fled away, seeing tremor of it, by some supernatural power. Next time, when they entered again, and polluted the temple, they all ran away when one of them was killed by snake-bite.

In the town, there lived a Brahmin named Kadwā whose cow used to pour milk on a Jain idol, in the nearby cave. The Brahmin told this story to one Jain Seth Dhanna Shah who dreamt about the idol of Parashvanath where this cow went, to pour its milk. After the search, on the fifth day of the dream, the idol was brought out, from the cave and installed in place of the old one in 894 A.D. (V.S. 951 and Vir Samvat 1421) and consecrated at the hands of Acharya Deva Gupta Suri of the monk order-Upkeshgachha. Later on, this idol was also replaced by the idol of Lord Neminath outside the main sanctuary (Garbha Griha), and Jeeravala Parshvanath idol was placed which is still there. The idol of Parshvanath is said to be of sand, mixed with milk. It is also said that the real idol of Jeeravala Parshvanath lies hidden somewhere here, in the earth.

Between 506 A.D. and 1324 A.D. (V.S. 563 and 1381, Vir Samvat 1033 and 1851) this place was visited by many Jain Acharyas from time to time. Many strange things were experienced by Jain monks and Jain laymen when they took vow, to rememder the name or to have Darshan (look) of Jeeravala Parashvanath, from their innermost heart. It is the only temple of Jains in India where 108 idols of Parashvanath, are found by different names. There is a Dharmashala and Bhojanshala attached with the temple, for the convenience of the pilgrims.

'Celestial Simla'
to
"The City of Sun-rise."

ABU TO UDAIPUR

Starting from 'Celestial Simla' (Abu) to 'The City of Sun-rise, (Udaipur), we come down to Abu Road station, 18 miles or 30 Kilometers to catch up the train for Falna Railway station which is only 99 kilometers away. From Falna, the private buses play to Udaipur, passing by Sadri, Charbhuja, Rajnagar, Kankroli, Nathdvara, Eklingji, after covering a distance of 105 miles (175 Kms). From Falna, we can also take the rail route via Marwar Junction, Mavli Junction to reach Udaipur which is only 263 kilometers. From this route also, we can go to Charbhuja, Kankroli and Nathdwara, by their respective stations which lie between Marwar Jn. and Mavli Jn.

The advantage of travelling by a bus or a private car, is that we can conveniently see the renowned places of pilgrimage and antiquity. From Falna, we come to Sadri (about 15 miles or 28 Kms) where there are 14 Jain temples and some of them are ancient and magnificent. From Sadri, at a distance of 6 miles, we find the famous temple of Ranakpur, in a remote valley piercing the western flank of Aravallies surrounded by natural scenery.

The temples of Ranakpur

The temples at Ranakpur are unique in architecture and design. *The Adishwar temple* was built by Sheth Dhanna Shah (Dhānak Dharnā Shah), in the form of Nalini-Gulma Vimān (a kind of heavenly aircraft which he saw in his dream. It took 65 years (1367 to 1432 A.D.) to construct this temple and its architect was Dipā Shilpi. It was erected during the reign of Rana Kumbha of Mewar—a great Builder of Forts and Temples, descending below Komulmer or Kumbhalgarh (the Rana's favourite Fort). "The foundation stone was so laid and the bases were so cleverly and mechanically filled that it could accomodate this big temple and on the base, the structure of three storeys with several pavilions. The 1444 pillars of all the pavilions were so beautifully and artistically carved that anyone who sees the figures in that beautiful piece of architecture, cannot but be impressed with the same. It is probably the most complicated and extensive Jain temple in India and most complete for the ritual of the sect. In the centre stands the great shrine of Adinath or Rishabhadev, the first Tirthankar, occupied by a quadruple image in white marble, surrounded by smaller shrines and domes, all encircled by a Bhamati or range of cells for images, each of which has a pyramid roof of its own. It covers altogether about 48,000 sq. ft. or nearly as much as one of the ordinary madiaeval Cathedrals. There are said to be 84 underground cells also."

Nearby, there is the *marble temple of Parshvanath,* with the main door in the north. It has a black stone image and its exterior is covered with good sculpture. The temple of Parshvanath is also known as Pātriyon kaā Mandir because of indecent nude form of its architecture. Close by is another temple of Lord Neminath, with its main entrance to the east. To the South-West of it, at a distance of about 150 yards, there is *Surya Narain Temple.* Its principal doorway is to the east. The image of Surya Narain or Sun-God, is a beautiful specimen of fine scultpural art. In its close vicinity, there are ruins which was once in the shape of a fort. If excavated by the Archaeological Department, a new light can be thrown on Ranakpur.

The famous architect, Fergusson has described the Ranakpur temple in these apt words "I know of no other building in India, of the same class, that leaves so pleasing an impression or affords so many hints for the graceful arrangements of columns in an interior".

Jain Gorwad Panch Tirth.

The Jain Panch-Tirth of Gorwad or the five Jain places of pilgrimage in Gorwad region, are Muchālā Mahavirji, Narlāi, Nādol and Varkānā, along with Ranakpur. After coming from Ranakpur to Sadri we motor to *Muchala Mahavirji*, at a distance of 12 miles, slightly diverting from the main road. The temple is situated in natural environment amidst hills and dales. The legend says that Rana Raj Singh of Mewar, came over this place for worship. He saw white hair in the saffron which he wanted to put on the idol. At this, he asked the Pujari and the latter replied that hair were of the moustaches of Lord Mahavir. The Rana insisted to see the moustaches. For this purpose, Pujari fasted for three days and pleased with this the protecting deity showed moustaches on the face of the idol. When Rana uprooted the moustaches, blood oozed out. After that time, the Rana showed great devotion and the name of idol was known as Muchala Mahavirji There is very fine carving in the interior of the temple, with two big black-coloured masonary elephants, standing outside the main door, one on each side. There is also a neat and clean Bhojanshala (kitchen) for the pilgrims. The temple is looked after, by the All India Jain Trust-Anandji Kalyanji Pedhi.

Narlai.

After plying 12 miles from here, via Ghanerav, we reach *Narlai*. At Ghanerav also, there are 11 Jain temples, the famous being that of Adishvar temple of the times of the famous king Samprati 'The Shah Jehan of a period two centuries before the Christian era'.[1] Narlai, is only 3 miles from Ghanerav. There are also 11 temples among them, the Adishvar temple is said to be about 1000 years old. The oldest temple is of Suparshvanath (the seventh Jain Tirthankar) having sculptural art. The Neminath temple on the hill is also famous. It is said that one of the hill temples was brought by a Yati, with his magical power. Round about Suparshvanath Temple, there were existing once, 2700 houses but now they are all lying in ruins.

Nadol.

Further, about 7 miles from Narlai, there is another ancient place called Nādol where once resounded every evening 999 bells indicating 999 temples. There are 10 Jain temples, the famous being that of Lord Padma Prabhu (the sixth Tirthankar), the idol being consecrated in V.S. 1681, (1624 A.D.), by Jaimal, the minister of Maharaj Gaj Singh of Jodhpur. The temple is architecturally beautiful. The popular Jain verses of '*Laghu Shanti Stavan*, were composed here in V.S. 300 (243 A.D.) by Acharya Mānadev Suri. Col. Tod, the famous historian of Rajasthan, found ample material from this place including hand-written scriptures (which he took away with him), and the family trees of the popular kings Shrenik and Samprati.

Varkana

From Nadol, at a distance of nearly 5 miles, another famous temple of Varkānā is situated. The temple is of Lord Parshvanath having 52 shrines. It was built in V.S. 1211 (1154 A.D.), with hand-some designs of carvings. The place is calm and quiet. There is Jain Dharmashala

1. Col. Tod : Annals and Antiquities of Rajasthan, 1957 edition pp. 721-723.

and a Jain High School. From Rani, this place is only 4 miles. Every year on Posh Bid 10, a mela or a fair is held within the precincts of the temple.

Nakoda Parshvanath.

From Rani, we reach, by train to Balotra Junction, on the Northern Railway, Via Marwar and Luni Junctions. The temple of Nakodā Parshvanath, is only 6 miles South of Balotra and is surrounded by bare hills which form its natural background. The private buses run, usually, at the train times. Nakoda, is an ancient place. In the 3rd century, there existed two cities-Virampur and Nakoda each 20 miles apart, founded by Virsen and Nākor sen respectively. In both the places, there were big Jain temples of 52 cells and their consecration ceremonies, were performed, at the hands of renowned Acharya Sthulibhadra but those temples were destroyed by Alam Shah. The consecration ceremony took place in V.S. 62 at Nakoda, at the hands of Acharya Mantung suri. In V.S. 909 (852 A.D.), there are said to be 2700 houses of Jains in Virampur and the idol which was kept hidden in Naghrida (Kalidrah), was installed in V.S. 1429 (1372 A.D.) at Virampur or Nakoda. This main idol at Nakoda is of Lord Parshvanath. It is 23 inches in height and black in colour. It is very attractive with its tutelary deity Bhairava. The people from far and near, visit the shrine and make offerings to Nakoda Bhairava, on fulfilment of their desires. Besides this main temple, there are the temples of Rikhabdev (Lachi Bai's temple) and Shantinath, besides 35 idols in the underground cell. There are few extensive Dharmashalas, in the compound of the temples, for the pilgrims to stay in. Every year, a grand mela or fair, is held on Pash Bid 10, the birthday of Lord Parshvanath.

Ghat Section.

Returning from Nakoda, by the same bus route, we entrain at Balotra and come to Charbhuja Road Station Via Marwar Junction and Phulad Junction. Between Phulad and Kamlighat, we pass through Ghat—Section. There are intermittent serpentine sharp curves and two big tunnels, as the train ascends from the plain below to the top of the hill. The lower plains of Marwar lying beyond Phulad, look vast and dim and present a beautiful landscape along with the natural scenery of the surrounding hill sides, to the onlookers, in a passing train. When ascending the Ghat Section in the rainy season, one feels amidst the beautiful valleys of Kashmir. The top of the Ghat section is 2155 ft. above Sea-level.

Charbhuja

The distance from Charbhujā Road to Charbhuja is nearly 18 miles, by a good coal-tarred road. It can be approached by bus also from Falna Station Via Sadri and Desuri, enroute to Udaipur. Charbhuja is a famous place of pilgrimage. The temple is said to be about 1000 years old. No date of its construction is available. It is dedicated to Charbhuja or four-armed divinity of the Hindus—Lord Vishnu. There is an inscription which relates that the temple was repaired in V.S. 1501 (1444 A.D.) by Lakshman, the son of Mahipal and the name of this village was Badri. A big fair is held every year in the rainy season, on Bhadrapad Shukla 11, when people from Mewar, Marwar and Malwa throng here in a large number.

Rup Narain

From Charbhuja, there is another temple of Rup Narain, in Sevantry village, 3 miles away. It is said to have been built at the same time as the temple of Charbhuja. This is dedicated to Rama and the other to Lakshman. The old original small temple is still, in existence. The present large temple is built over it with massive pillars in carving, in V.S. 1709 (1652 A.D), at the cost of Rs. 5,1001, by Merta Jagat Singh of the family of Rao Duda. Opposite to it is a small temple, some 600 or 700 years old containing well-carved out images of Vishnu, Brahma, Sun and four-faced Shiva. There is a fine Kund said to have been built by Chand Bai, sister of Maharana Bhimsingh.

Kumbhalgarh

Returning to Charbhuja from Rup Narain we proceed to Kumbhalgarh, by another route which is 16 miles away, via Majera and Kelwada. The bus goes only upto Kelwada from where Kumbhalgarh is only 3 miles and from Udaipur direct, it is 40 miles. It is 3568 feet above sea-level and stands on a craggy mountain crowned with splendid building of the Palaces. It commands a fine view of wild and rugged scenery of the Aravallis and the sandy deserts of Marwar. It is a very cool place in the summer season. It is defended by a series of walls with battlements and bastions built on the slope of a hill and contains a domed palace and buildings reached through seven gates, along a winding approach. It was built by Rana kumbha in 1458 A.D., on the side of a more ancient castle which tradition ascribes to Samprati, the Jain prince existing in the 2nd century B.C.

The principal buildings on the fort are Nilkanth Mahadev, Vedi, Mammadev temple and Kartargarh. Nilkanth Mahadev is older than the other buildings on the fort. Its unique design with its slender fluted pillars and Greecian style, has been described in Tod. Gauri

Shanker Heera chand Ojha denies this fact and claims it not to be earlier than the 2nd century B.C. Moreover, the temple of this sort with high pillars is rare to be found in Rajasthan. Vedi is situated, just near the Hanuman Gate of the fort. It is a sacrificial temple built by Kumbha, perhaps, to commemorate the completion of the fort. Col. Tod describes it a three—storeyed Jain temple. It is a beautiful building of much architecture which was recently renovated by Maharana Fateh Singh. It is the only remnant to be seen of the ancient sacrifical places of India.

Mammadev temple and kund were built in 1460 A.D. by Kumbha, below the fort. It was interesting because it contained four large slabs covered with inscriptions giving the history of Mewar from the time of Gohil, the founder of Mewar family to Rana Kumbha now preserved in Museum, at Udaipur. Near the temple is a large Kund or reservoir. Close by it, is the Chattri of Prithvi Raj—the 'Knight-errant of Mewar."

In the central open space of the fort, lies the inner fort named Kartargadh crowned with a palace built by Maharana Fateh Singh after pulling down the old palace built by Kumbha. A portion of the old building still remains below the new palace which includes the historical portion said to have been occupied by Prithvi Raj mentioned above.

Besides this, there are three old Jain temples,[1] containing handsome Jain image in white marble of V.S. 1608 (1551, A.D.) (2) *Bavan Deola*—the Jain temple of 52 cells—a fine specimen of a large temple of the same date as Kumbha's fort and (3) beautifully carved Golera Jain temple having a samll beautifully carved Jain Pittaliya temples, north of the fort, once containing the brass image as indicated by its name.

Parasu Ramji:—There is wild and romantic place, in the descent, two miles south-west of the fort, by the name of Parsu Ramji. It is approached on foot as the country is very rugged. It can be ascended also from the foot of the mountain, by Marwar side. The shrine of Parsuram Mahadev is situated in a small cave above which is a curious cleft in the rock from which water constantly tickles below, on the image.

Rajsamand:—Returning by the foot-path to Kelwara and from there to Charbhuja, by bus, we reach Rajnagar which is 22 miles form Charbhuja. In Rajnagar, there are two important places to be seen. One is Rajsamand lake, built by Maharana Raj Singh between 1662 and 1676 A.D. to alleviate the sufferings of his starving population at the cost of Rs. 10507, 584 It is the oldest known famine relief work in Rajasthan. The lake is 4 miles long and 1¾ miles broad and 55 ft. in depth. the dam forms an irregular segment of a circle nearly 3 miles long, the northern portion of which, is about 200 yards long and 70 yards broad and is entirely faced with white marble of Rajnagar. Along the front, a flight of steps descends to the waters edge while jutting out into the lake are three marble pavilions, with their pillars and roofs, decorated with the figures of The Sun, chariot, gods, dancing figures, pigeon-fights etc, all skilfully and artistically carved. On the bund stand five Torans (arches) the marks of charity dispensed in gold and silver as weighed against the person of Maharana Raj Singh. This beautiful portion of the bund is callad '*Nau-Chowki*. On the bund, there is an inscription engraved on twenty-five large slabs which contain the history of Mewar from the earliest time, down to Maharana Raj Singh. The whole is a beautiful work of human skill and a fine specimen of Mewar architecture. On both the ends of *Nau-Chowki*, stand the hills on the top of which are Dayal shah's temple and the palaces of Maharana Raj Singh. The latter are in ruined condition though some of them have been repaired recently. The other notable place, is the Jain temple of Dayal Shah.

THE JAIN TEMPLE OF DAYAL SHAH

This was built by Dayal Shah, the then Prime Minister of Rana Raj Singh. It cost him the same amount as was spent in the construction of Rajsamand bund. The temple is of large dimensions with walls all round. Its spire was partly destroyed by Maharattas and replaced by a round tower. It is said that there were nine storeys the reflection of which, used to fall upon a village named Kunwāria, some 6 miles from this place. Today, there are only two storeys existing. The upper storey of the temple, commands a fine view of the Rajsamand lake and the plains beyond. It also contains the idols of four Jain Tirthankars one in each direction. The lower or ground storey has fourfaced idols of Shri Adinath which were installed in 1732 V.S. (1675 A.D.). The carvings of the temple are fine and delicate. The temple is managed by a Jain Trust of Udaipur. At the base, there are old and new Dharmashalas for the convenience of Jain pilgrims, facing the road running between Rajsamand and Kankroli.

Kankroli

From Rajnagar, we come to Kankroli, at a distance of about a mile and half, passing by the motor bus-stand. Kankroli town is also approached by the rail route from Charbhuja Road Station to Kankroli station from which Kankroli is only $1\frac{3}{4}$ miles. Kankroli contains the temples of Dvarakadhish-one of the seven forms of Lord Krishna. The idol was brought from Mathura and installed here in 1676 A.D. The guardian of the temple, is one of the descendants of Vallabhacharya—the Vaishnava spiritual Guru. The temple is situated on the hill overlooking the lake Rajsamand. It looks grand and beautiful from the distance, across the lake. It is an important place of pilgrimage for Vaishnavas. The Dharmshalas are situated adjoining the temple and also at the base of the hills.

Nathdwara or 'Apollo of Mewar'

From Kankroli, we come back to Motor bus-stand, from where Nathdwara is about 10 miles. It is 7 miles from Nathdwara Railway station. It is situated, on the right bank of the river Banas. Nathdwara is famous throughout India as a great place of pilgrimage for Vaishnava community. It has one of the most famous temples in which is enshrined the image of Lord Krishna or better known as 'Shri Nathji' which is popularly said to date from the twelfth century B.C. This image was placed by Vallabhacharya in a small temple at Mathura in 1495 A.D. and was moved to Govardhan in 1519 A.D. About 150 years later, the image was brought over here. When persecuted by Aurangjeb, Rana Raj-singh gave shelter, by setting apart a village named Śihad in 1671 A.D. The building of the temple is simple in style but there is grace, design and harmony. The guardian of the temple is termed 'Gosain Maharaj' and is the head of Vallabhacharya sect. The full size image of Lord Krishna is very imposing and attractive specially when adorned with ornaments valued at couple of lakhs of rupees. The rush of pilgrims is heavy on Janmashtmi (Bhādra Badi 8) and Annakuta day following the Diwali festival, when Dharmashalas nearly a dozen of them are fully occupied. Besides the main shrine, there are other temples of Shri Vithal Nathji, Shri Navnit Lalji and the temple of Madan Mohanji.

Haldighati

From Nathdwara, as we proceed towards Udaipur we may take a turn from about 2 miles, to see Haldi-Ghati, which is 13 miles from Nathdwara. This is a historical place—the ancient battlefield where was fought the battle between Raja Man singh-the General of Emperor Akbar and Rana Pratap of Mewar. It has been denominated by Col. Tod as 'The Thermopolae of Mewar'., which was irrigated with the best blood of Mewar. It is an old heroic place of picturesque scene where Rana Pratap held his brave massacre driving the Moghul prince, on 7th July 1576 A.D. Every year, during the Pratap Jayanti celebration (the birth-day anniversary festival of Rana Pratap which falls on Jyeshta shukla 3, according to the Hindu calendar) a fair is held here. Two miles from Haldi-Ghati, is the memorial of the well-known charger 'Chetak' of Rana Pratap, on the bank of a rivulet.

Delwara

About 13 miles from Nathdwara, on Nathdwara-Udaipur road, stands Delwara—an important place of historical research and antiquarian interest. To the south on a conical peak, is the temple dedicated to goddess Rathasen or Rashtrasen. There are three ancient Jain temples called Vasahi, two dedicated to Lord Rikhabdev and one to Lord Parshvanath. They are not older than the year 1407 A.D. The queries of the antiquarians show that the town was once flourishing with rich merchants of Jain community and had been the seat of Jain monks, the famous being Som Sundar (1393 A.D.) and Muni Sundar (1421 A.D.). The latter composed here at Delwara, the well-known verse 'Shanti karana stavana', to ward off the malign disease known as 'Marki'. There, were once, 300 Jain temples and the town was known as Devkul-

Pattan'. There is rich antiquarian material, lying under the heaps of earth and stone.

Bappa Rawal

Further on the same road, about 2 miles from Delwara, in a jungle is Bappa Rawal's Chattri, containing a figure of Bappa, (the founder of the kingdom of Mewar) and an image of Vishnu. A stream from the Kund above the temple, runs through it. The spot is altogether very lovely and rcmantic and is known as 'Bappa Rawal.'

Eklingji

About 2 miles from this place is 'Eklingji—a religious place. It is also famous as "Kailashpuri"—the abode of Shiva—the family deity of the rulers of Mewar. The large temple of Eklingji, in the middle of the enclosure, was originally built by Bappa Rawal but has thrice been repaired, the last time by Rana Raimal (1473 to 1509 A.D.) It is also held that this temple was built on the site of 72 celled Jain temple of four-faced idol of Adinath, the first Jain Tirthankar, as is evident from the miniature idols found on the panels above the sanctuaries. There are the ruins of another Jain temple also, near the big tank, on the other side, further from Eklingji village.

It is said to be built, about the year 728 A.D. The shrine is of white marble and ample dimensions, under an open vaulted temple supported by columns and fronting the four-faced divinity is the bronze bull Nandia of natural size. The temple is of unusual design, having a double storeyed porch and sanctuary, the former covered by a flat pyramidal roof composed of many hundred circular knobs and the latter roofed by a lofty tower of more than ordinary elaboration. Inside the temple, is a four-faced image of Mahadev, made of black marble, the God being worshipped, under the epithet 'Eklingji' that is, with one Lingam. It is said that nowhere in India, the God Mahadev is worshipped with so much pomp and show and according to the rituals as here. There is an inscription of hundred couplets engraved by Rana Raimal which throws light on the history of Mewar as well as of the temple. A picturesque lake lies in the vicinity and the numerous other temples stand nearby out of which one built in the sixteenth century by Meera Bai, being of singular elegance.

Nagda

At a short distance of about a mile, there is the ancient capital of Mewar, known as Nagda or Naga-hrada, founded by Nagaditya in the 6th century. It is connected with Bappa Rawal's infancy and his miraculous relations with the sage Harit. Here the Maharana's ancestors ruled for seven generations till the time of Bappa. It had faced the fury of Muslim invaders several times, the most famous invasion being in the Thirteenth Century by Altamash, between 1222 and 1229 A.D. The ruins of this ancient capital are rich in Vishnu, Shiva and Jain temples. The important temples are the Sas-Bahu pair, said to be as old as the eleventh century. They are most beautifully carved and adorned with artistic figures and sculpture, in the very best taste, dedicated to Vishnu. The temple of Sas (mother-in-law) is larger, with a swinging Toran or archway in the front while that of Bahu (daughter-in-law) in the north is smaller. The larger temple is a perfect gem of its kind and is not surpassed by any old building in Mewar, not excepting Badoli.

The temple of Adbudji

The Jain temples known as Khuman Rawal's temple

and the temple of Adbudji, are important among others. The former is of curious type as having two mandaps and the latter is remarkable only for the great size of images, the largest that of Lord Shantinath, being 9 feet. This giant image was built by Oswal Jain, 'Sārang' in 1437 A.D., during the reign of Rana Kumbha. From the inscriptions found, it has been concluded that these temples are earlier than the 13th Century and some of them are certainly not later than the 10th Century. The Padmavati temple was built in the fourteenth Century.

"THE CITY OF SUN-RISE"
Udaipur

Introductory

It is one of the most important cities in India. There is nothing between Madras and Northern India, quite like Udaipur. It is most beautiful among the beauties; the grandest even amid the grandeur of Rajputana with its snow-like palaces and pavilions, with its flower gardens and shady groves, with its islands and exquisite lakes. It seems to the visitor a fitting frame-work for a dynasty of immemorial age, for incidents of romance and daring. It appears as if the inventive genius of man and symphonic harmony of nature have genially conspired together to make Udaipur, a perfect model of beauty. Due to its ancient history, superb beauty and natural romance, the city has been, rightly, called as "The Venice of India" or "The city of Sun-rise" and "The city of Enchantment". Recently, after independence of the Country, it has been named as 'The City of Institutions' as many important institutions have grown up in Udaipur. No other city in Rajasthan, can surpass in natural scenery. It is unrivalled and can be compared with Kashmir alone.

Much can be said about its glorious history but it would be inappropriate to mention in this book. It remained very recently the capital of Mewar State—the land which produced a galaxy of heroes in quick succession, who magnified the name of Rajasthan, all over the world. The history of the rulers of Mewar who trace their origin from the Sun-God, is one continuous heroic struggle, for freedom of thought, religion and country against superior forces. The acts of heroism, fortitude, magnanimity of spirit and love of independence, as illustrated from time to time find no parallel in the chronicle of any country. This si the soil in which the flowers of Rajput Chivalry sprangto life.[1]

The city stands on the slope of a low ridge, the summit of which is crowned by the Maharana's palace and to the north and west the houses extend to the bank of a beautiful piece of water known as The Pichola Lake. The city is girded on its three sides by high ramparts (now broken at some places) having circular bastions at intervals and on the western side by the lake. The principal gates—Surajpol to east, Chandpol towards north-west, Hatipol to the north, Delhi Gate or Delhi Darwaza to the north-east, and Kishanpol to the south, are all remarkable in their way as specimen of architectural fortification. Surajpal gate has been modernized by laying out a circular park, named after Rana Udaisingh who founded Udaipur and erecting an oval shaped gushing fountain beyond it, from which we catch the glimpse of the city of Udaipur.

There are good many Dharmshalas, Sarais and hotesl inside and outside the city, the important being, Fateh-Memorial (State Sarai) and Radha Madhava Nivas Dharmshala, (outside Surajpol), Jain Dharmashala (just outside Hathipol), Ajanta Hotel (outside Hathipol) Lake—view Hotel, Laxmivilas Palace and Anand Bhawan (near Sarupsagar) Alka Hotel and Tourist Bungalow (in Ashoknagar) and Garden Hotel (Gulab Bagh) and Lake Palace Hotel (Pichola Lake).

1. The readers interested in the history of Mewar, can read with advantage, the author's book. 'A Brief History and Administration of Mewar, with a Foreword by T. Vijaya Raghavacharya Price As 12 (.75 Paise) which can be had from, Jodh singh Mehta, Maldas street, Udaipur.

We start from Fateh Memorial to visit the important places of interest round and inside the city. The tongas are largely available here and private taxis can also be arranged from some of the hotels. The buses also ply from the bus-stands outside Hathipol, Surajpol and Chetak Circle for excursions and travel, in the suburbs of Udaipur. The visitors and tourists are advised to contact Tourist's Information Bureau (Tourist Bungalow Phone No. 405) and Tourist Guide Service (Chetak circle phone No 326) for detail information to guide them properly, to see Udaipur and the places outside Udaipur.

Shital Nath Jain temple and others

Starting from Fateh Memorial and entering the city, by Surajpol, we come to the Clock-Tower, in the heart of the city, passing through the main markets. Near the Clock Tower, there is a big Jain temple of 52 cells of Lord Shital Nath (the tenth Tirthankar) profusely decorated with the multicoloured glass work. It is said to have been founded on the same day when the foundation of the Royal Palaces was laid in V.S. 1624 (1567 A.D.). The temple commands an extensive area having two big Upasaras (abodes for the Jain monks). The main Upasara, was the principal seat of Tapagachha Jain Sadhus (yatis) and it has also a good library of the old printed and hand-written books. The Maharanas of Udaipur used to pay high respects to Shri Pujyaji (the chief head of this Jain monk order) whenever he paid visit to Udaipur. The temple has also fine glass-work and colour-painting. Near the clock tower, a bye-lane leads to another temple of Chotta Shital Nath in Jadiyon ki Ol and further to it, is the temple of Lord Rikhabdev, with beautiful white marble image. There are, altogether 36 Jain Svetambar temples inside and outside Udaipur city which could be shown by a guide available at Jain Dharmashala, Hathipol.

Jagdish Temple

Coming back to clock tower, we proceed to Jagdish temple, at a great height (80 ft. from the road side). It is reached by ascending the flight of steps. It was built by Maharana Jagat Singh in 1628-1653 A.D., at a cost of Rs. 15 lakhs. It stands on rectangular platform about 25 feet abóve the ground. The temple consists of a pyramidal spire (Shikar), a vestible (mandap) and a porch. It is three-storeyed building with fifty pillars each in first and second storeys. The central temple is ornamented with excellent carvings and bold figured friezes. Round the main temple, there are small and well-conceived shrines in four corners dedicated to Ganesh, Shiva, Sun and Shakti (Goddess). There is a sanskrit inscription, on both sides in the porch dated 1651 A.D., giving a detailed account of the reign of Maharana Jagat Singh, by a Pandit Krishna Bhatt. In front of the principal shrine, there is a huge brass image of Garuda. It is one of the largest and most venerated temples of Vishnu, in Northern India.

The Maharana's Palaces

At a short distance to the south of Jagdish temple, on the same road, there are the old Palaces of the Maharana 'an imposing pile of buildings, running north and south, in front of Rai-Angan (a long rectangular courtyard)'. Fergusson has described them as the largest in Rajputana and in outline and size, a good deal resembling Windsor. "The chief apartments to be seen, in the interior are Choti-Chitra Shali (a court-hall inlaid with brilliant mirror mosaics of peacocks), Suraj Chopād (the hall of the Sun), Pitam-Niwas (the Palace of Delight), Manak-Mahal (The Palace of Rubies) Moti Mahal (The Palace of Pearls) Chini-ki Chitra Shali (The court and pavilion with finely inlaid mirror and porcelain work) Dil Khusal Mahal (the palace decorated with mirror work of painted and gilt background) and Chandra Mahal (The Moon Palace), on the top of the building commanding a fine view of the city and the surrounding country. Above them all is Bādi-Mahal or the Garden Palace of white marble stones with flower-beds, a few trees and a fine reservoir in the centre.

Connected with these palaces, are the residential palaces of the present Maharana which are known as Shambhu Niwas and Sajjan Niwas, both situated on the Pichola lake, with a big Durbar Hall—a spacious hall, enclosed by a rectangular gallery with a beautiful balcony jutting out. The beauty of these modern buildings has been described in these words, for its architect.

"Who when all was done should have been tenderly dropped into the lake at the foot of its walls." These palaces are not open to the visitors.

The Pichola Lake

This is the loveliest and most beautiful lake of Udaipur, on the west, reached by descending from the slopy stone-studded path near the Badipol (the main entrance of the Maharana's palace) to Navaghat. Originally, the lake was built by a Banjara or a grain-carrier at the end of 14th Century and finished by Rana Udaisingh who founded Udaipur, by shifting his capital from Chittorgarh. It is $2\frac{1}{4}$ miles long and $1\frac{1}{4}$ mile broad, fed up by a big stream from the western mountains. The lake is encircled by massive white palaces, dark and bare hills, rows of bathing ghats with throngs of people, marble temples with their flags flying high in the air and the rich mansions, with balconies jutting out in water which however, they may look at close quarters, gain from the distance and the bright Sun, at least the semblance of beauty.

At early dawn, before the Sun has risen behind the high white palaces, the soft pearl grey light lends a touch of fairy and in the stillness, every temple and palm tree and every mountain peak is mirrored to perfection in the quiet water. Beyond, the palaces are few and finally give way altogether before the jungle. At intervals, the lake narrows almost to a melting point. At such places, it is spanned by the pretty arches of ornamental bridges.

The Island Palaces.

'And every now and again, there occur little islands, each a beautiful sylvan retreat crowded with palaces or pavilions of glittering white stones. Among these pretty islands, the most famous are Jagmandir and Jaganivas—the natural gems of Udaipur. Mohan Mandir and Natini-ka-Chabutra are very small places, inside the lake, the later having a legend of its own.

Jaganivas Palace—It was built by Maharana Jagat Singh II in 1754 A.D. It is a collection of small apartments, courts, and gardens. The new Sajjan-Nivas palace containing swimming bath and fountains, some highly ornate and marble-floored halls, inlaid with coloured glass frescoes, describing tigers, beasts, a large glass bed, has been built in excellent native taste.

In one of the palaces, there are historical paintings on the walls. It is one of the prettiest palaces of the world and covers an area of 4 acres. The lake Palace Hotel, is enshrined in this palace island. The glass furniture is attractive and amazing. A visitor can see this palace island, by purchasing one rupee ticket, for the boat service.

Jaga Mandir--Towards the southern side of the lake, there is Jagamandir which can be seen on the payment of Rupees two, as charges for the boat ticket. This island palace was finally completed by Maharana Jagat Singh I (1628-1652) and named after him. It is famous both historically and for its picturesqueness. On the eastern end of the island is the edifice built most beautifully, to provide shelter to prince Khurram (later on Emperor Shah Jahan) when in revolt against his father Jehangir. During the Indian Mutiny in 1857 A.D., it was used as an asylum for several European families, by Maharana Swaroop Singh.

The marble has long since lost its snowy whiteness but the yellow dome and elephant cupolas rising above the dark green of mango trees and palms still lend to the palace a touch of fairyland. And indeed, there is much that reminds one of fairyland or suggests one of the country of Peter Pan. The upper apartment is circular in construction, being about 21 feet in diameter. Fergusson thought, it was the prettiest room he had ever seen or known in India. "Its floor is inlaid with black and white marbles, the walls are ornamented with niches and decorated with arabesques of different coloured stones in the same style as the Taj at Agra, though the patterns are Hindu and dome is exquisitely beautiful in form. A room built of twelve enormous slabs of marble, Shah Jahan's throne sculptured from a single block of serpentine and the little mosque dedicated to Kapuria Baba, a Muhammedan Saint are other objects of interest on the island."

About these two spots it has been said;-

"The low yet extensive island fringed with marble piazzas enclosing luxuriant orange-gardens interspersed with sombre cypresses; towering palms and gilded minarets shooting up here and there; the whole resting upon background of the dark and lofty Aravallis, forms a scene unsurpassed by any other in India." Fergusson, the famous antiquarian, has written about these two islands that "the only objects in

Europe to be compared with them are the Baromean islands in the Lago Maggiore but I need scarcely say their Indian rivals loose nothing by comparison. They are as superior to them as Duomo at Milan is to Buckingham Palace. Indeed I know of nothing that will bear comparison with them anywhere."

Khas-Odi. At the southern end of the Pichola lake is Khas-Odi or a shooting box. It is now, not a shooting box but a small palace with beautiful surroundings, approachable by a boat or a car or a tonga. The place is very charming and very peaceful.

From Khas-Odi, we take the road route and reach Samor garden, passing by Dhud-Talai (milk-Tank). It is a small garden belonging to the Maharana of Udaipur, containing a temple of Neelkanth Mahadev and a stair-cased well. Above it is Badipāl or the big embankment of the Pichola lake.

Sajjan Niwas garden-Gulab Bagh.

In front of samor, there is Sajjan Niwas garden or Gulab Bagh one of the biggest and the best gardens of India, covering an area of about 100 acres. In the garden, there are green trees, flower beds, a museum and a zoo. In the museum, we see very fine collections of antiquities and curios. The public Library attached to it, has a large number of books and illustrated manuscripts on Indology, History and Archaeology. Besides it, there is a Public reading Room, in a spacious hall. The museum, Public Library and Reading Room all the three are housed in the big and beautiful building called Victoria Hall, in front of which there are green lawns. In the month of Shrāvan, during the rainy season, fair is held on every Monday.

Ekling—gadh or Machla Magra

Between Samor and Sajjan Niwas garden, there is road which leads towards Ekling-gadh or Machla Magra, towards the extreme South. On this small fish-shaped hill, there are some pieces of cannons including a big one. Formerly, the guns were fired from this place, at midday and midnight, the sound of which was heard through the city and even beyond it. It is 2,469 ft. above the Sea-level and joined with the walls of Kishanpal mentioned in the beginning. Enormous piece of ordnance is said to have been mounted in 1764 A.D, when Scindia laid siege to Udaipur. From the top of the hill, a beautiful view of the Pichola lake and the low-lying city of Udaipur could be obtained.

Today, we end our journey and return to Fateh Memorial, by the road between Samor and Sajjan Niwas garden, passing by Rajasthan Mahila Vidyalaya and Surajpol.

THE SECOND ROUND

Ahad

From Fateh Memorial, we take the second round to Ahad, passing by Town Hall, Rajasthan Vidya Peeth and Delhi Gate. A bye-road from Delhi Gate, reaches Āhad, going through Ashoknagar. It is two miles from the Delhi Gate. Ahad is famous for Mahasatia or Cenotaphs of the rulers of Mewar, their family members and the nobles etc. The imposin g Chattri at Mahasatia is that of Maharana Amar Singh I who died in I620 A.D. Close by is Gangodbhava or the sacred reservoir (Kund) with a Chattri or cenotaph, probably of Gandharva Sen, the brother of the famous king Vikramaditya of Ujjain. It is said to have been founded in about 950 A.D. by Rawal Allat of Mewer, on the ancient ruins of Tambavati

Nagri, where lived the ancestors of Vikramaditya, before he took possession of Ujjain. The place is of particular interest to archaeologists and research scholars. The excavations so far conducted by the Archaeological Department of Rajasthan have revealed the ancient Chalcolithic culture of Rajasthan of nearly 3750 years. There are very ancient temples and vestiges of immense mounts formed by ashes of volcanic eruption containing sculptures, pottery and coins. In old inscriptions and Jain literature, its name is Aghātpur. There are four old Jain temples of nearly 1000 years, having fine carvings.

Sethji ki Badi and Chougan Mandir.

From Ahad, we return to Chetak Circle by the same route but move straight passing by Tourists' Bungalow, Central Post Office and the General Hospital. Behind the Chetak cinema and in front of the General Hospital, there is a fine big Jain temple by the name of *Sethji Ki Badi*, having flower beds and green trees in the compound. It has a fine idol of Lord Parashvanath and the beautiful Chitra-paṭa of Śammet-Shikhar. From Chetak cinema, the road goes straight to Saroop sagar lake, In between, we see Chougan or Bhopal stadium and Chougan kā Mandir to our right hand side. The Jain temple of Chougan has a special feature of having a big marble idol of Padma Nabh Prabhu (the soul of the king Shrenik) who would be the first Jain Tirthankar of the future twenty-four Tirthankars. This is the only temple in India where the future Jain Tirthankar is worshipped.

The idol with a height of 95 inches contains beneath an inscription of V.S. 1819 (1762 A.D) the year when this idol was installed. The area of the temple is extensive having three other temples of Shantinath, Mahavir in one line and a shrine containing four-faced idols of Jain Tirthankars, in the upper storey of the temple of Shri Padma Nabh. The shrine on the top of the temple, commands an excellent view of Saroopsagar lake, just near-by and the surrounding hills. In the compound of this temple, there is Shri Vijaya Shanti Shiksa Bhavan, Secondary school, a club and Jain Bhojanshala.

Saroopsagar lake.

A little further from Chougan Mandir, we catch the glimpse of Saroopsagar lake, connected with the Pichola Lake, by an arched bridge built by Maharana Saroop Singh (1842 to 1861).It has a long bund to the east, with a circular building known as *Saroop Sagar Ghat.* Close to it, is the Lake View Hotel. As we advance, we find Anand Bhavan and the State Dak Banglow where there are arrangements for lodging and boarding at moderate rates. Adjacent to it, is Laxmi Vilas Palace Hotel, overlooking the famous lake Fateh Sagar, provided with all modern amenities. Both Anand Bhavan and Laxmi Vilas Palace Hotel, command beautiful view of Fateh Sagar Lake and the surrounding hills beyond. Our second journey, ends here.

THE THIRD ROUND

Fateh Sagar Lake.

The third round, from Fateh Memorial to Fateh Sagar lake, begins, on this very route near Anand Bhavan which we have left. Walking down a few paces, we catch the glimpse of crystal-watered lake of Fateh Sagar which is joined by a water channel with Saroop Sagar lake and is hidden among the bushy hills. The zig-zag balustrade of stones on the road between its waters and hills lend a charming spectacle to the eyes. It is famous as '*Fateh Sagar Drive*'. It is pleasant, specially in the morning and evening when the rising and setting sun imparts a golden tinge to the surrounding atmosphere. The coal-tarred road, running parallel to zig-zag balustrade, passes by Moti Magri where Rana Udai Singh lived here. It is also supposed that Rana Pratap also lived in these palaces, (now in tottering condition), in his childhood. Pratap-Smārak or Memorial monument to Pratap—'The Robert Bruce of India, the great soldier and the First Freedom Fighter of our country has been constructed and a life-size statue of Rana pratap, on his famous charger '*Chetak*' was inaugurated on the 11th October 1967. Further, on the right, we see the Municipal Rock Garden, full of rich flower plants and luxuriant green trees, onlooking the placid waters of the lake. The beauty of Fateh Sagar is that of a peaceful natural scene. The boating can also be had on petty payment, from the bank near the Rock Garden, in the lake and also to the two islands inside it.

Nehru Park—In front of the Municipal Rock garden, the first oval-shaped island, is at a distance of 1400 feet, from the waters of Feteh Sagar Lake. This island, has been named as '*Nehru Park.*' It may also be called as 'Enchanting Park' of 'The city of Lakes'. Recently, it was inaugurated, by Sardar Hukum Singh, the Governor of Rajasthan, on the 14th November, 1967. This park, was constructed, at the cost of Rs. 6 lacs. Like, the Island Palaces of Pichola, this new artistic island garden, on-looking the ancient Moti Mahal of the world-famous Rana Pratap, takes pride, in its glamorous beauty. It seems, as if, it is paying respects, with great devotion, to the brave son of the universe. This island garden, encircled by the burnished, silvery and crystal-like waters of Feteh Sagar, looks like a heavenly spot, in the midst of lovely surrounding hills.

It is 772 feet long from North to South, and 19 feet

broad from east to west. Its area is about 41 acres or 1, 96,020 sq. ft. which includes 62000 Sq. ft. of charming and fragrant flower garden and 2,000 Sq. ft. of multi-coloured fountains. Also, a zig-zag Lily-pond, in 35, 000 sq.ft; exhilarates, the hearts of the visitors. Around the park, there has been constructed, a circuitous roving belt of 19, 900 Sq. ft, with artistic design, for looking to all the places on it. In the near future, the Kirloskar Company who laid the jet fountains here, is also contemplating, to turn them into musical jet fountains. If it so happened, then, the beauty of this celestial spot, would be enhanced all the more and Nehru Park would become, the main centre of attraction, for the tourists.

To the north-eastern corner of this island, in the midst of water, there is a small island—a rectangular platform which has been nick-named as, *Kirloskar Platform*. In fact, Nehru Park, is a unique specimen of human handicraft, in the lap of mother Nature.

Finally, we reach its bund known as Connaught Bund', as it was formally laid by the Duke of Connaught in 1889 A.D. It is about 2800 feet long and 50ft. broad with white spired towers and a marble pavilion in the middle. It was built by Maharana Fateh Singh, and hence it is known as *FatehSagar*. The whole resting on the background of blue sky, presents a sight unsurpassed in beauty and splendour. The lake is 1½ miles long and 1½ miles broad with an average depth of 35 ft. In the rainy season, the waterfall of the lake, towards the southern corner of the bund exhibits varied and multi-coloured reflection when the coloured electric lamps and tubes, are placed, on the outward side of the wall over which water falls. A big local fair is also held in the month of Shravan Amavasia (15th day of the Hindu month Shravan) for males and on the following day for the females when all around the lake, the hills look green and pleasant.

This fair is known as the Hariyali Amāvas Mela. The fair is held outside the northern gate of the road running parallel to the bund. Adjoining the Mela-ground is a conical-shaped hill on which stands the temple of Neemuch Mata (a goddess). The people ascend the hill to pay visit to the goddess and also to enjoy the landscape of the surrounding country and the lake below, on the Mela day. The whole view round the lake is really so lovely and enchanting that an excursion to it, either in the morning or in the evening is quite a treat.

Sajjangadh

From Fateh Sagar Bund, a road also goes towards west to Sajjangadh—the fort built by Maharana Sajjan Singh. (1874-84). It is about 3 miles west of Udaipur city, upto the top of the hill. It, is 1100 ft. from the plain level and 3100 ft. above sea-level. The airy marbled white palaces on the top, look like a diadem worn on the head of the rocky hill. The edifice is massive and commodious, commanding the most excellent and lovely view of the surrounding smoky hills, crystal-water lakes and snow-white palaces.

Badi Ka Talab

Near it is Badi Ka Talab, built by the mother of Maharana Raj Singh (1652-80) at the cost of Rs. 2.60.000. It is $1\frac{1}{4}$ sq, miles in area and 75 ft. deep. It is about 6 miles from Udaipur by a good road. There is a big T.B. Sanatorium near it. The embankment on the lake is 600 feet long. This lake provides a picture of quite beauty and restful atmosphere in a wild setting of wooded hills.

Saheliyon Ki Badi

Another road from the Mela-ground near Neemuch Mata hill goes to the east, passing by Vidya Bhavan a private Public High School imparting education on modren lines. From this road, a bye-road passes towards the south which leads to *Saheliyon ke Badi or slave girls' garden* which is beneath the Fateh Sagar lake. Inside it is, a reservoir surrounded by four black-marbled Chattris, in the four corners and one white one in its centre, from the terraces of which water gushes out from the inner fountains and also from the beaks of the birds placed upon them, in the form of torrential rain. Adjoining it, is the palace built by Maharana Fateh Singh and outside the palace compound, there are beautiful fountains and an oval-shaped water pool strewn with green lotus-petals on which fall the water-drops like pearls, from the tusks of four marble elephants, on its four sides. The whole scene looks simply charming and beautiful. Round about the palace walls, there are green fruit trees and the rose flower-beds. This small garden, with luxuriant verdure and lovely fountains, appears like wonderful place in a fairyland. After seeing this enchanting garden, we return to Fateh Memorial, from which we started, passing by Mohata Park and General Hospital.

THE EXCURSIONS FROM UDAIPUR

Rikhabdev or Kesariyaji

From Udaipur, a trip to Rikhabdev, about 40 miles south of Udaipur, is worth while undertaking by a private taxi or bus. The place can be reached from Udaipur city Railway Station to Rikhabdev Road Ry. Station (146kilometres) and from there to Kalyanpur village (½ mile) on foot and from Kalyanpur to Rikhabdev by private bus covering a distance of 6 miles. The scheme to construct direct road from the Railway Station to Rikhabdev is under consideration.

Rikhabdev is famous, as its name indicates, for the temple of Lord Rikhabdev, the first Jain Tirthankar even though the Vaishnavas claim the Lord as their eighth Avatar. "The Temple of Shri Rikhabdev, is a Svetambar Jain temple and is, at present, being managed by the State of Rajasthan".[1] This temple is well renowned in India, as 'Kesariya ji, the name derived from Kesar or saffron being put on the idol of Rikhabdev, profusely. The Bhils who also worship the idol, call it as 'Kālāji', due to its black image. The town is also called *Dhulev* as the Bhil Dhula, protected and worshipped the idol, at this place. The Bhils take also the solemn oath by uttering the name of Kalaji and after this they do not tell a lie. No inscription about the origin of this idol has been found as yet, but it is believed that it is very ancient one and its history goes to remote antiquity. It is said that this very idol, existed during the times of Rāvan, in Lanka from whose clutches, Sita the wife of Rama, was liberated after she had look or Darshana of this idol. It is also the belief of the Jains that this idol was worshipped in Nandan Vana and from there Ravan brought to Lanka or Ceylon and from there Rama brought it with him, after his conquest of Lanka. It was installed, at Ujjain, by the king Shripāl and his wife Menāsundari Later on, it remained in Bāghad region for sometime and from there, it came out lying hidden in a tree, after having appeared in a dream to Dhula Bhil. The tutelary deity of Kesariyaji, is so strong and influential that the desires of the pilgrims, have been seen fulfilled, after taking vow to visit the place and to worship the idol. It has been seen that the pilgrims besmeared the idol with Kesar or saffron equal to the weight of their child born, after taking the vow and its fulfilment.

1. From the judgment of the 30th March 1966, Sajjan Lal & others vs State of Rajasthan (D.B. civil Writ Petition No. 501 of 1962. Rajasthan High Court, Jodhpur).

The temple was repaired in the 14th and 15th centuries. The oldest inscription is of V.S. 1481 (1424 A.D.). The sanctuary of the temple was built in the 14th century. The temple is also famous for its architecture and sculptural beauty. This is the temple of Bavan-Jinalaya having 52 cells round this temple. In front of the main temple, before the courtyard, there is the idol of Marudevi Mata, the mother of Lord Rikhabdev, being seated on marble elephant. There are many Dharmashalas managed by Bhandar Dhulev of Dewasthan Department of Govt. of Rajasthan. Besides the office of Bhandar Dhulev, there is Pedhi of Keshariyaji Jain Svetambar Sangh and a Bhojanshala by the name of Shri Jain Svetambar Bharatiya Shri Sangh Bhojanshala.

About a mile from the temple is an old beautiful place, on Rikhabdev-Kalyanpur road, by the name of Pagliyaji, where the foot-prints of Lord Rikhabdev are placed in a handsome Chattri and are worshipped Just adjoining the compound wall of the Chattri, there is the trunk of a tree enclosed by masonary structure from where it is believed that the idol came out. In front of it, is a newly constructed hall wherein is enshrined the idol of Lord Rikhabdev also. The atmosphere of Pagliyaji, is calm and peaceful, surrounded by green trees, neighbouring hills and a rivulet, flowing nearby.

A big fair is held every year at Rikhabdev on Chaitra Badi 8, on the birth-day of Lord Rikhabdev, when the procession of the Lord proceeds from the temple to Pagliyaji.

Jawar

On return journey from Rikhabdev to Udaipur. a road from Tiddi (20 miles from Rikhabdev) goes to Jawar where there are zinc, lead and silver mines existing in the fourteenth century and now, being worked out by the Hindustan zinc Limited—a Government of India undertaking, with modern mechanical process. The ancient town of Jawar, lies in dilapidated condition containing many Jain and Hindu temples. There existed here a Moti Bazar and near it the temple of Shantinath built in 1421 A.D. by Dhan-Pal Shah, a Porwal Jain. There are seven Torans or arches indicating that seven lakhs of rupees were spent over it. Near it, is an old Sās-Bahu temple. The most attractive temple, at some distance from the ruins of Moti-Bazar, is that of Lord Vishnu built by Ramadevi (the daughter of Rana Kumbha and wife of Rao Mandlik Bhama of Saurashtra (Girnar in Kathiawar) in the year 1447 A.D. There is a fine kund below the temple of Shiva. The Jawar Mata temple, in close vicinity, is ancient and beautiful under the old shady trees, containing an inscription of 1548 A.D. and another inscription in the temple, is of V.S. 1554 (1497 A.D.) on black stone. Jawar Māla, is a historically famous place on the hill, about two miles from Jawar. It is said that Rana Pratap lived here in the cave when engaged in guerilla warfare against the mighty Moghul forces of Emperor Akbar. This is said to be the place where a piece of bread was snatched by a cat from the hands of the daughter of Rana Pratap. The author has seen this place, about 35 years back and there were seen four holes of the hooks from which, it is said, the cradle of Rana's daughter, was fastened.

Dhebar—Jai Samand Lake

From Jawar, we return to Udaipur and make another journey to the south-east of Udaipur to Dheber or Jai Samand Lake, It is connected by a good metalled road of 32 miles from Udaipur. It is one of the biggest artificial lakes of the World, covering an area of 21 Square miles. It is 9 miles broad and the greatest depth is 102 ft. with the circumference of 30 miles. It was built by Maharana Jai Singh in 1685 A.D. There are 7 islands, inhabited by the Bhil Meenas. On the bund (1202 ft. long and 116 ft. in height and the breadth at the base 70 ft.), there are six beautiful Chattris and a temple of Shiva in the centre. At the northern extremity, there is a palace with court-yard while on the southern end, there is a pavilion of twelve pillars. On the hills to the south, are gorgeous palaces commanding a beautiful view of the lake. The visitors can see the lake by motor-boat. The mountaneous jungle scenery round about the lake is simply charming. Diving and swimming in the deep waters of the lake are good pastimes.

A JOURNEY TO CHITTORGARH

Udai Sagar Lake.

A journey by rail, from Udaipur city to Chittorgarh (117 kms) Via Udai Sagar and Bhupal Sagar, is worth undertaking, to acquaint with the natural and historical background of Mewar. After moving 16 kms., we get down at Udai Sagar Ry. Station and walking down about 2 miles we come to Udai Sagar Lake. Its massive bund built of huge stones, is very high, different from the bunds of other lakes. It was built by Rana Udai Singh, in five years between 1559 to 1564 A.D. On account of its lovely sight, Maharana Fateh Singh built fine palaces on Medi Magri, a small hill nearby. The lake covers the area of about 4 square miles. It is 2½ miles in length, 2 miles in breadth and 35 feet in depth. The Ahad river falls into it and in the rainy season when the lake is filled up to the brim, the surplus water falls from the Nala-(waste-weir) very loudly and presents a beautiful scene, forming the source of the river Berach. This place is a fine spot for picnics. The bund is also historically important, being the place, where a feast was served to Kunwar Man Singh of Amber—the General of Emperor Akbar and the hot words were exchanged between him and Rana Pratap. This episode, later on, became the immediate cause of famous battle of Haldighati. It is also said that in 1680 A.D. Maharana Raj Singh routed the forces of Emperor Aurangjeb, near about this place.

Kareda or Bhupalsagar

After seeing the sight of Udaisagar lake, we return by

the same road and catching up the train from Udaisagar Ry. Station, we get down at Bhupal Sagar Ry. Station, at a distance of 55 kilometres. From the Railway station, the village Kareda is hardly a mile. Here is the famous Jain temple of '*Kareda Parasnath*', a huge and magnificent edifice. It was built in the last decade of the 16th century. It possesses very fine architecture, both inside and outside the temple. "The domes are of nearly equal diameters, about 30 feet each and about 40 feet in height. There is a splendid colonnaded vestible at the entrance, richly sculptured which gives a grand appearance to the whole edifice." One great peculiarity of this temple construction, was that once in a year on Pos Badi 10 (when the fair is held) the reflection of the Sun's rays, fell upon the face of the idol of Lord Parshvanath, passing through the big entrance of its compound wall and the main entrance of the temple. But on account of raising its parapet, this phenomenon does not occur now. The idol is of black marble which is very imposing and attractive. It bears an inscription of V.S. 1656 (1599 A.D.) when the idol was installed in the temple. The oldest inscription of V.S. 734 (677 A.D.) beneath the image and the other of V.S. 1039 (982 A.D.), on the side of the door-way, are other inscriptions in the temple. The temple is said to have been originally constructed by Simandhar Shah in V.S. 1024 (967 A.D)[1] when the village known at that time as the town of Kerapur Pattan, was a great commercial centre, and prosperous, being ruled by Raja Raj Mewali. Pethad Shah, the minister of Junagarh, built a temple here and his son Jājan Shah repaired it. Another version is that this temple was originally built by Pethad Shah, and not by

1. Muni Gyan Sunder : Bhagwan Parshvanath Ki Parampara Kā Itihās, Part II pp. 1562.

Simandhar Shah[1]. There is a big Dharmshala inside the temple compound and there is arrangement also for the Jain pilgrims, of a bullock-cart by Kareda Parshnath Karkhana, to bring and take them to Bhupal Sagar Ry. Station.

Beside the temple, there is Bhupal Sagar tank of 2 square miles recently constructed by Maharana Bhupal Singh, for irrigation purposes. On the extremity of its bund, there is a Dak Bungalow on high altitude which presents a lovely sight of the low-lying waters and far-off plains. Near the Railway Station, there is a Sugar Factory by the name of 'The Mewar Sugar Mills Limited'.

CHITTORGARH—*the Cradle of Chivalry and Culture*

Preliminary—Last but not least in importance, is the ancient fort of Chittor where fierce and bloody battles were fought incessantly for centuries together, for the protection and independence of Mewar, against foreign aggressions. It is the living monument of the ancient rulers of Mewar. "Every brick and stone on this hill speaks eloquently of valour, patriotism and sacrifice and every temple and tower points to its ancient culture. It had not only been a scene of battle but had also remained a great seat of learning and literature, art and architecture, rhyme and religion."

It is no longer possible for me to narrate the ancient history of the fort and the significance of all its monuments in this book which has been primarily meant for Abu or Celestial Simla. The readers interested to know more about its ancient history and the full details of all its moun-

1. From, 'Sukrit Sagar, verse 45 pp. 21.
'नागदा नागपुरे नासिक्यवटपद्रयो सोपानके रत्नपुरे कोरटे करहटके
॥४५॥

ments, would do well to read our book "Chittorgarh'.[1] However, I would try to mention important monuments in a nut-shell for the guidance of the tourists.

The Ascent

The fort is constructed on a hill, three and a quarter of mile long and a little more than half a mile broad. It is a fish-shaped hill of about 400 or 500 ft. in height. The summit of the fort is approached through seven gates, from the base of the hill, each gate being associated with the episode or history of its own. Beginning from Pādan Pol, the first gate of the fort, on the ascent, we come to Rampol, the last gate, decorated with elaborate Hindu designs, after passing through Bhairon Pol, Hanuman Pol, Ganesh Pol, Jodla Pol and Lakhsman Pol. In front of Padan Pol, to the left is *Bagh Singh's memorial*—the spot where Bagh Singh, the great-grandson of Rana Mokul, was killed, in the second siege of Chittor in 1534 A.D. by Bahadur Shah of Gujarat. Between Padan Pol and Bhairon Pol, a foot-path leads to Jharna or a water-fall which descends from the cliff below Gaumukh or Cow-mouthed reservoir. This place surrounded by thick and shady trees, is beautiful. Between Bhairon Pol and Hanuman Pol, there are two Chattris or Memorials of Jaimal and Kalla, the immortal defenders of the fort who were killed here, during Akbar's siege in 1567 A.D.

Round the Fort:—Entering the main gate viz. Ram Pol, we see in front of it, a *Chabutra or a platform of Patta*, the illustrious hero of the last sack who fell fighting in 1568 A.D. Akbar was so much impressed by the chivalrous act of Patta that he

1. "Chittorgarh—'The cradle of Chivalry and Culture,' By Balwant Sinha Mehta and Jodh Singh Mehta, with a Foreword by Dr. Satya Prakash, Director of Archaeology and Museum, Rajasthan Price Rs. 3. To be had of:—Sahitya Kuteer, Ren Basera, Hospital Road, Udaipur.

carved out his effigy in stone and placed it on the gateway of his palace at Agra. From here, we proceed towards south and see the *Temple of Tulja Mata* built by Banvir, the nephew of Rana Sanga, (1535-1540 A.D.) with the riches of the weight of his person. Further on the same road, we find to the left, *Nau Lakhā Bhandar or Nine Lakh Treasury,* a huge circular bastion, built in the sixteenth century to keep the treasure of Mewar. Near it is Naulakha magazine or nine apartments to keep big old cannons. Near the Top Khana, there are lying Buddhist stupas of fine carving. In front of the magazine, there is the house of Bhāmā-Shah, "the Saviour of Mewar" who offered his amassed wealth, at the feet of Rana Pratap and also fought along with him on the battle-field. Tracing back our steps and reaching again by Naulakha Bhandar, we see on the left, *Shrinagar Chanvri* a richly carved Jain temple, with geometrical Jali (lettice) work. It was rebuilt in 1448 A.D by Velaka, the son of Kola, the treasurer of Rana Kumbha. Opposite to the Jain temple, are the Palaces of Rana Kumbha which were planned and worked with excellent taste and design. It is typical of the domestic architecture of the Rajputs. In close proximity to Kumbha's Palace, we look to a modern double-storeyed building—Fateh Prakash Mahal, with four towers on each corner, built by Maharana Fateh Singh in 1907 A.D., at the cost of about 6 lacs of rupees. To the south-west of it, is Sat-Bis Deora or a big Jain temple of twenty-seven shrines built originally in 1448 A.D. and repaired in V.S 1998 (1941 A.D.) having profuse carving and adorned with images.

A path from the tri-junction of the roads, in front of this temple, goes to the right and leads to the *Temple of Kumbha-shyam* consisting of a shrine, a mandap, a portico and open circumbulatory passage (Pradaksina). It was built by Rana Kumbha, in 1448 A.D. (1505 V.S.) and dedicated to Varaha (the boar incarnation of Vishnu). In the same compound is '*Mira Bai's Temple*' built in the year 1524 A.D. by Rana Sanga, for the worship of his daughter-in-law-the famous Meera.—the Sweet-singer of India. A trust has been established, for the repairs of this temple, in which the idol of Meera- her Girdhar gopal (Lord Krishna) would be installed.[1]

Jai-Stambh or The Tower of Victory.

To the west of it, is the most prominent monument of the fort, namely Jai-Stambh or The Tower of Victory, erected by Rana Kumbha, to commemorate his victory over Mohammed Khilji of Malwa, in 1446 A.D. On it, are represented the symbols of every religion. It can be compared only with Kutub-Minar at Delhi, though the latter is much higher but of very inferior character. The tower is about 120 feet high, standing on the basement of 47 ft. square and 10ft, high. It has nine storeys through which passes a staircase of 157 Steps. The chief architect of this unique building was Sutradhar Jaita. The tower took seven years to be built, and cost 90 lacs of rupees.

To the south-west of the tower, is *Mokulji's Temple* which was originally built in the 11th century by Raja Bhoja and later repaired by Rana Mokul in 1428 A.D. It is a beautiful, carved stone temple. The shrine contains a

1. It is said that Maharana Udai Singh, installed, the idol of Meera's favourite deity Lord Shri Krishna, in the Royal Palace of Udaipur after her death, by getting it, from Dvarika—the famous place of pilgrimage. Another version is that this is not the same idol, now placed, in the Royal palace, which Meera used to worship. It had been removed and taken to a Jagirdar of Nurpur (on the hilly border of Kangda) by a family of priests of Kapasan village, on account of incessant attacks on Mewar, by the Moghuls. But the latter version, has been denounced by Muni Jin Vijaya Ji a well-reputed antiquarian, of Oriental learning-who has established, in the light of his recent research on Meera that this is the very same idol of Meera's favourite god, Girdhar Gopal which, is, at present, enshrined, at the Royal Temple of Udaipur.

colossal image of Tri-Murti Shiva, Brahmā, and Vishnu. It is also known as Sammidhesvar Temple, dedicated to Sammidhesvar Mahadev. It contains two inscriptions-one dated 1150 A.D. referring to Solanki Kumarpala who visited Chittorgarh in that year and the other dated 1428 A.D. relating to Rana Mokul. Close to the entrance of this temple, is layer of ashes where Rani Karmavati, the mother of Rana Udai Singh, performed Johur with 13.000 ladies, that is, burnt themselves into the burning fire, to save their chastity, before their husbands who were on the battle-field. Around Mokulji's temple is *Mahasati or Royal crematory*, from the Southern gate of which, we descend a long flight of steps and come to the sacred *Gaumukh or Cow-mouthed fountain* and a reservoir below it, known as Sās-Bahu Kund.

Further, on the margin of *Patta Jaimal Tank*, are the *houses of Patta and Jaimal*, mentioned above, with beautiful projected balconies, decorated with blue enamel. On the margin of the tank, there is a water spring by the name of *Surya-Kund* from where an armed horseman came out for the defence of the fort, as related in tradition.

The temple of Kalka Mata.

Beyond these palaces, there is an ancient *Temple of Kalka Mata*. It was originally a temple dedicated to Sun-God but now there is seated Kalka Mata or the goddess Kalka. It is the most ancient building on the fort, built in the eighth century. The sculptures of the temple, are superior in taste than those in other temples of Mewar not excluding those of Nagda and Badoli. Proceeding to the south of this temple, we see some ancient ruins of the *House of Salumber* where once lived Chunda—"The Modern Bhisma', the son of Rana Lakha, who being the eldest son, renounced his claim to the throne of Mewar, for the sake of cherished principles.

Padmini's Palace

Then seeing the grave of *Nav-gaza Pir*-the grave of a Musalman nine yards in height nearby, we come to *Padmini's Palace*, a large and beautiful building by the name of Padmini—the daughter of Raja Hamir Singh of Sinhaldvipa and the wife of Rana Ratna Singh who was extremely beautiful, wise and brave. She rescued her husband from the captivity of Allauddin Khilji, by her clever device. With the beauty and chastity of Padmini, all the memories of the fort are fragrant.

A road from Padmini's Palace goes to the South and on the west of it, we see *the Haveli of Rampura* and to the east of it is *Chougan* or a big military ground 1200 by 450 feet. Then, we see further *chitrang Mori Tank*, built by Chitrang, the Maurya King. To the west of it, are the ruins of *the Palaces of the Maurya kings* built in the 7th century, before the advent of Bappa Rawal in Chittor. Beyond Rampura Haveli, to the east is *Bhāksi or prison house of Mohmmad Shah the Sultan of Malwa* who was kept in captivity here.

Mohur Magri or Chittori Hill.

From the tank of Chitrang-Mori, to the southern bastion, overlooking the semi-detached hill of Chittori, the distance is about three quarters of a mile. The southern bastion is called *Chittori Burj* from which *Chittori Hill* is 1500 feet below. It is historically known *Mohur Magri*, raised up artificially by Akbar who paid during the siege a Mohur or a sovereign each for every basket full of earth thrown over. The gold mohurs of the time of Akbar, have been found here and deposited in the State Treasury. From here, we turn to north-east and passing by *Raja Tila* or a high raised platform where coronation ceremonies of the Maurya kings were held, we come to the extreme north of the fort where there are *The domes of Gora and Badal*, the uncle and cousin of Rani Padmini who fought bravely against the army of Allauddin Khilji and were killed. The road to the north passes by the *House of Rinmal* and leads to *Bhimlat* Kund or reservoir where Bhim, the hero of Mahabharat, dashed his foot in chagrin when he could not build the fort, hearing the feigned cry of the cock, by the contrivance of Yogi Nirbhaya Nath.

On the western side of the northern road, there is a large carved stone *temple of Adabadji*, having three-faced image of Lord Mahadev built in 1394 A.D. by Rana Raimal.

Kirti Stambh or The Tower of Fame

Advancing further by *Suraj-Pol* or The Sun Gate and *Nilkanth Mahadev*, we reach, *Kirti Stambh or The Tower of Fame*, built in twelfth century by a Bagherwal Jain Jeeja, and dedicated to Adinath or Rishbhdev. It is smaller than Jai Stambh, being 76 feet high and 37 feet in diameter at the base, on the square platform of about 10 feet. It is a singularly elegant specimen of architecture. From base to summit with seven storeys, it is adorned with sculptures and mouldings. Each storey is differently carved from others. The lower level is called Hansh Peeth, then follows, Sinha-Mukh Thar, Gaja-Thar, Nava-Thar.

From Kirti Stambh, a mid-path goes straight towards the north passing by Lakhota Bari and Kukreshwar Kund, to Ram Pol. Another road turns towards south-west of Kirti Stambh and meets near Sat-Bis Deora, passing by The *Temple of Muniji and Bhim-Godi—a* staircased well ascribed to Bhim, one of the Pandavas.

Returning we come to the neat and descent *temple of Charbhujaji*, built in V.S. 1924 (1867 A.D.) by Rana Shambhu Singh. This is also known as *Shambhu Kunj*, after the name of the Rana. From the temple of Charbhujaji, we return to the main road and proceeding, first to the north and then to the west, we come to three temples, among them the temples of Annapurna, Banamata are conspicuous. To the north of them is the Kund or tank of these goddesses, known as *Mataji ka Kund*. On the western margin of this Kund, there once stood magnificent *temple of Kukudeshwar Mahadev* of which nothing remains except a pillar, in the south-west corner of the Mandap. The present temple was re-built by Rana Kumbha. Col. Tod found here, an inscription of V.S. 811 (755 A.D.) relating to the temple. Further to it, are found the Jain temples in which are enshrined the idols of V.S. 1198, 1501, 1553 and 1660. The idol of V.S. 1501 is that of Lord Shanti nath—the sixteenth Tirthankar.

The Palace of Ratnasingh and Ratneshvar Tank

To the north of the Jain temple, is the *Palace of Ratna Singh* known as the *Palace of Hinghal Ahāria*, built by a member of Duager family—an off-shoot of the branch of Guhilot family, before the siege of Allauddin. Being in tottering condition, it was re-constructed by the Rana Ratna Singh, hence it is called the Palace of Ratna Singh. To the north of the main gate of this palace, there is a temple of Shiva, by the name of *Ratneshvar Mahadev* and in front of it is a beautiful lake known as *Rataneshvar Kund*.

Lakhota Bari and Kukreshvar Kund

A footpath from the gate of the above palace, goes to *Lakhota* Bari—the small northern gate of the fort. It is so-called because nearly a lakh of men were killed at the gate. After seeing Lakhota Bari, we return to the main road and proceeding further, to the east of the road, there is a large and deep reservoir called Kukreshwar Kund, built by Raja Kukreshwar in 755 A.D. Traditionally, it is connected with Bhim who dashed his foot in despair, on hearing the feigned cry of cock by Yati Nirbhaya Nath. The place from which Yati imitated the cock's cry, is said to be Kukreshwar Kund. From this Kund, we come back to Rampol, after a full round of the fort.

NAGARI

Before we end the description of the fort of Chittor, we cannot forget an ancient place called Nagari seven miles from Chittorgarh. Here once existed the Republic of Rajasthan, the Capital of which was Madhyamika.[1] This republic was founded by Sivis who migrated here after facing the first known invasion of India by the Greeks. In Nagari, have been found very recently the relics of the pre-historic age which easily remind one of the earliest Indian civilisation of several thousand years back. The ruins of the capital of Sivis remind us of its prosperous past of the early historic period. The ruins of Nagari are seen, stretching far off from the present inhabitation and among them are to be seen the old Jain, Buddha and Hindu temples. A votive Stupa from Nagari is still seen lying under a tree, at a little distance from Nav-Lakh Bhandar. Inscriptions of the period as early as 2nd Century B.C. have been found here. One of the epigraphs in Brahmi script, inscribed 84 years after the Nirvan or salvation of Lord Mahavir and found at Berli near Ajmer, mentions in it, the ancient town of Madhyamika—modern Nagari village, near Chittor. This inscription is one

1. The Berli inscription of 443 B.C. mentions Madhyamika as the capital of Shivi Republic.

"माध्यमिका शिविजनपदस्य"

of the few very old, if not the oldest, not only in Rajasthan, but also in the whole of the country. Three inscriptions have been found in the script prevalent near about 2nd century before Christ and one of them mentions in two lines about some construction undertaken with a view to show compassion to all creatures.[1]

I commenced this book, from the ancient Abu and end it, also, at the ancient place of the earliest Indian Civilisation taking my readers, in between, to the various religious and conspicuous places of antiquity and historical importance, in that part, of Rajasthan, where Nature has also played an equal roll, in making it a beautiful and heavenly region of India.

1. "स वा भूतानाम् दयाधम कारितां"—
शुङ्ग कालीन माध्यमिका नगरी से प्राप्त शिलालेख
—G.H. Ojha's Udaipur Rajya ka Itihasa pp. 358

INDEX

B

J

K

N

S

CORRIGENDA

Page	*Line*	*Incorrect*	*Correct*
3	11	Sahasmal	Shesmal
7	16	stirking	striking
8	21	Old site	Old site with
10	8	samet Shikar	Samet Shikar
12	29-32	Anand Ghariji	Anand Ghanji
14	8	Central Police Training College	National Police Academy
	10	State Teachers' Refresher Centre	State Teachers' Refresher Training Centre
30	4	Jain idol	Jain idols
47	30	udayaprabha	Udayaprabha and
51	3	Adeshvar	Adishvar
52	11	Khareatar	Kharatar
58	5	farmer	former
	7-30	Adeshvar	Adishvar
64	14-28	Bhramati	Bhamati
65	11	Surija	Suriji
	22	Chief	Chiefs
70	19	1933	1533
71	7	Bhatrihari	Bhartrihari
	13	Dudnavavdi	Dudhavavdi
	22	Central Police Training College	National Police Academy
76	30	,,	,,
77	17	,,	,,
82	5	August	July
86	15	Adeshvar	Adishvar
	28	Laymen	laymen
88	22	of	(delete)
	22	image, Rikhabdev	image of Rikhabdev
	24	bhramati	bhamati
90	6	Arassor	Arasoor
92	8	has	had

94	19	lies	lie
96	13	as	(delete)
	22	Yaksa	Yakshas
103	2	ex-ruler	rulers
	9	ex-ruler	ruler
105	4	witl	with
	21	Hamirgah'	Hamirgadh'
111	13-14	Shridattā	Shridatta
	16	Shridatta	Shridattā
113	4	Lahar	Lahir
115	3	Tajpal	Tejpal
	12	Tej Mahal	Tāj-Mahal
	20-21	Sāsu-Bahu	Derāni-Jethāni
117	25	he	The latter
120	31	temple	temples
122	14	mohur	mohurs
123	2	minister	ministers
	12-13	their elder brother Luning	Tejpal's son Luna Singh
128	25	kaā	kā
129	6-7	Tirth	Tirthi
131	31	Pash	Posh
143	3	si	is
	13	Hatipol	Hathipol
	17	named after	where is to be installed a statue of
150	8	Kishanpal	Kishanpol
153	34	19 ft.	192 ft.
154	29	Cletric	electric
	20-21	folces.	forces.
162	28	Raja Raj Mewali	Raja Rajmal Mewali
169	3	yrmy	army
170	19	Duager	Dungarpur

1. The exterior view of Vimal Vasahi P. 16

2. The sculpure of famous Jain Achārya Shri Hir Vijaya Suri—the preceptor of Moghul Emperor Akber, in cells No. 23 and 24 of Vimal Vasahi P. 22

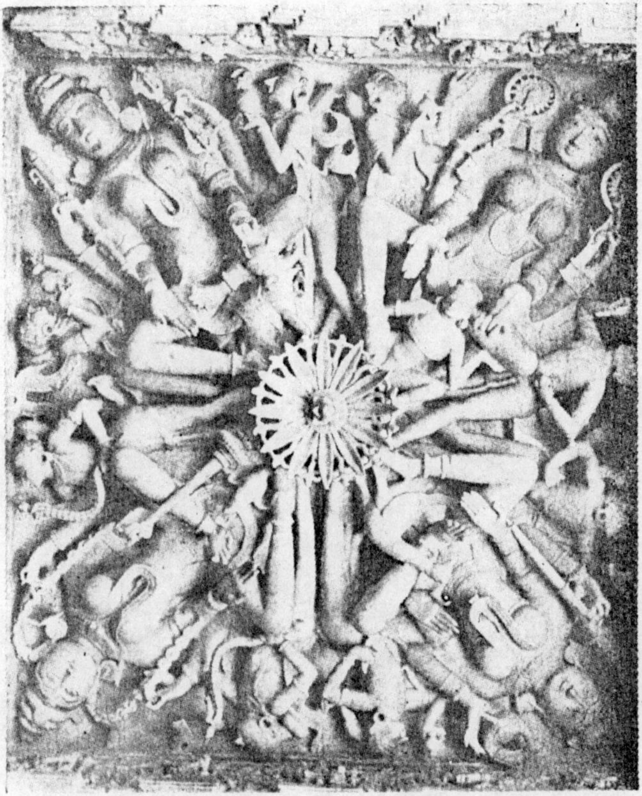

3. A unique carving of four goddesses with a lotus flower in the middle, in the ceiling opposite to cell No. 44 of Vimal Vasahi P. 23

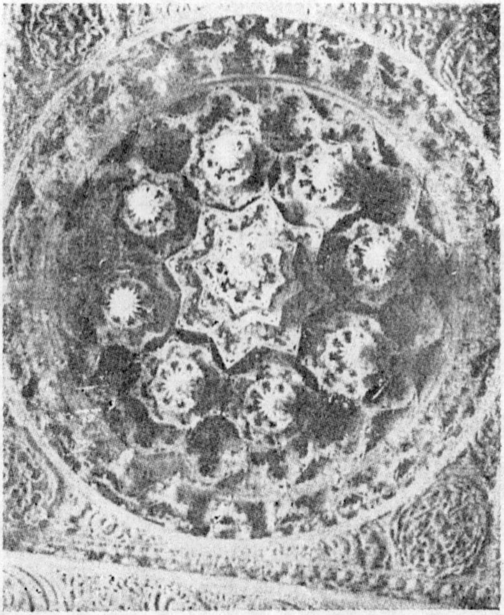

4. A domed ceiling depicting exuberant carvings, near the principal door of Vimal Vasahi P. 26

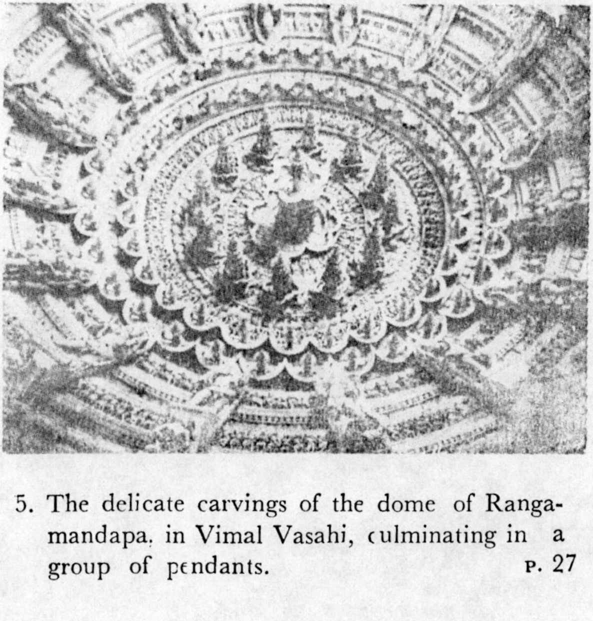

5. The delicate carvings of the dome of Ranga-mandapa, in Vimal Vasahi, culminating in a group of pendants. P. 27

6. The portion of richly and marvellously figured pillar in Rangamandap of Vimal Vasahi P. 27

(*By courtesy of Seth Kasturbhai Lalbhai, Ahmedabad*)

7. The Derāni-Jethani Gokhda (niche) of fine workmanship and minute chiselling, in Luna Vasahi P. 39

8. The ceiling panel of 108 dancing poses, on lotus-petals, to the south-west of Rangamandap, in Luna Vasahi P. 42

9. Guru-Shikar—The highest peak of Abu P. 59

10. The general view of the Jain shrines of Achalgarh P. 63

11. The general view of exquisitively beautiful Nakhi Lake, Mount Abu. P. 72

12. The Sun-set Point, Mount Abu. P. 76

13. The figures of dancing goddesses, beautifully carved out, on a pillar of Adishwar temple, Rānakpur. P. 128

(By courtesy of Seth Kasturbhai Lalbhai, Ahmedabad)

14. The bird-eye view of Nākoda Pārshvanath temple, in natural background. P. 131

15. The Jain temple of Dayāl Shah, Rājsamand. P. 136

16. The large temple of unusual design, having a double-storeyed porch and sanctuary, Eklingjī p. 139

17. The general view of the city of Udaipur, from Surajpal gate, with gushing foūntains.

P. 142

18. Jaganivas Island Palace, Udaipur—a collection of small apartments, courts and gardens. P. 147

20. A Jain temple of Ahad (Aghātpur) Udaipur having fine carvings of nearly 1000 years. P. 151

19. Jagmandir Island Palace, Udaipur, famous both historically and for its picturesqueness. P.148

21. The image of the big idol of shri Padma Nabh Swami-the future first Tirthankar in Chougān Jain temple, Udaipur P. 151

22. The zig-zag balustrade of stones on Fatehsāgar Lake, running parallel to the main road, known as "Fatehsāgar Drive", Udaipur.

P. 152

23. The life-size statue of Rana Pratāp —the First Freedom Fighter of India, riding on famous charger, Chetak, at Pratap-Smārak, Motimagri, Udaipur. P. 153

24. Nehru Park—The Enchanting Park of glamourous beauty in the crystal-like waters of Fatehsāgar, Udaipur

p. 153

25. The oval-shaped water-pool in Saheliyon-Ki-Bādi, Udaipur, strewn with green lotus-petals on which fall the water-drops like pearls, from the tusks of four marble elephants, on its four sides. P. 156

26. Dhebar or Jaisamand Lake—one of the biggest artificial lakes of the World, with six beautiful chattris and a temple of Shiva, in the centre. P. 159

27. Chittorgarh—The general view of the fort. (The copyright of Archaeological Survey of India—By courtesy of its Director General.) P. 163

28. Chittorgarh : The Palaces of Rana Kumbha, planned and worked out with excellent taste and design. P. 165
(The copyright of Archaeological Survey of India—By courtesy of its Director-General)

29. Chittorgarh : Sat-Bis Deora, having profuse carvings and adorned with images P. 165
(*The copy-right of Archaeological Survey of India—By courtesy of its Director-General*)

30. Chittorgarh : Jaya-Stambha or The Tower of Victory, having nine storeyes and representing the symbols of every religion. P. 166
(The copy-right of Archaeological Survey of India— By courtesy of its Director-General)

31. Chittorgarh : Mirābai's temple—the temple of famous Meerā—'the Sweet-singer of India' P. 166
(*The copy-right of Archaeological Survey of India—By courtesy of its Director-General*)

32. Chittorgarh : Padmini's Palace—a large and beautiful building. P. 168
(*The copy-right of Archaeological Survey of India—By courtesy of its Director-General*)